All Dogs Great and Small

All Dogs Great and Small

What I've learned training dogs

Graeme Hall

7
Ebury Press, an imprint of Ebury Publishing
20 Vauxhall Bridge Road
London SW1V 2SA

Ebury Press is part of the Penguin Random House group of companies
whose addresses can be found at global.penguinrandomhouse.com

The information in this book has been compiled as general guidance on dog training. It is not a substitute and not to be relied on for professional advice. So far as the author is aware the information given is correct and up to date as at 21.12.2020. The author and publishers disclaim, as far as the law allows, any liability arising directly or indirectly from the use, or misuse, of the information contained in this book.

First published by Ebury Press in 2021

www.penguin.co.uk

A CIP catalogue record for this book is available from the British Library

ISBN 9781529107449

Printed and bound in Great Britain by Clays Ltd, Elcograf S.p.A.

The authorized representative in the EEA is Penguin Random House Ireland, Morrison Chambers, 32 Nassau Street, Dublin D02 YH68

Penguin Random House is committed to a sustainable future for our business, our readers and our planet. This book is made from Forest Stewardship Council® certified paper.

For Axel and Gordon, without whom none of this would have happened

This book is a work of non- fiction based on the life, experiences and recollections of the author. In some cases names of people, places, dates, sequences and the detail of events have been changed to protect the privacy of others

Contents

Part Two

Foreword by Julian Norton

I had a busy morning on the farm, pregnancy testing cows with my arm in the place where most farm vets put them if we don't know what else to do. As we worked our way through the herd, Eric, the farmer, related a strange problem about his adolescent springer spaniel. It was a problem the likes of which I had never come across before. He explained the situation, I think looking for a solution.

'My new dog has a strange problem. I don't know what to do and it's getting rather embarrassing. Every time the telephone rings, he *ejaculates* all over the kitchen floor. Any ideas what might be going on in his head? What do you think I can do? It's not normal, is it? Have you ever heard of this sort of thing before?' He emphasised one word with unnecessary vigour.

After I had pulled my arm out of the cow and picked myself up from the floor, having collapsed with laughter, I regained my composure and a small degree of professionalism.

'Well, Eric, I've never heard of that before,' I confessed, between chortles. Eric was not so amused, because it was getting to become a messy problem, as well as an embarrassing one. 'Maybe you should change your ringtone?' was the only advice I could give.

As vets, we often see dogs – and sometimes cats, rabbits and ferrets – with behavioural issues. Some are funny, like Eric's spaniel, but some are really serious, causing anxiety to the canine and concern to the owner. Many of these problems are deep-seated and complicated and not easily investigated by X-rays or blood tests; harder to cure than a deep-seated skin infection or a disease of the prostate gland. Even a broken bone or a torn ligament has the chance of a once-only surgical repair. We must remember that dogs are both pets – fully assimilated into the family of humans and an integral part of the pack – but also reasonably primitive beings, not a million miles away from a wolf. My first dog, Paddy the border terrier, who was cuter than any other dog I've enjoyed the company of, quickly reverted to his inner wolf when he got smell of a deer or hare. He was fired with adrenaline, but even with this and powered by the 'red mist', his little legs stood no chance of ever catching his quarry.

So, the job of adjusting, balancing and juggling the complicated canine brain, which strives to advance itself to match the rest of its pack on the one hand and yet is obsessed by pheromones and anal scents on the other, is beset on both sides by conflicting inequities. I do not envy the challenges that Graeme is faced with each day.

I felt privileged to have been asked to write this foreword. Graeme and I have lots in common. We are both from Yorkshire; we have both found an unlikely home on Channel 5, a home where we can both share our love and work with anyone who cares to watch; we both earn our living by working with animals, which is a privilege in itself. The circumstances of our first meeting (and how we came to talk about me doing the foreword to this book) were unusual. In London, at Television Centre, Wood Lane, one damp day in February, we met outside the green room. I had just appeared with Holly and Phil on *This Morning* to promote my most recent book: *A Yorkshire Vet – The Next Chapter*, the fifth in a line, which represented my latest obsession. Graeme had been promoting the next series of his popular show. I think *his* animals had behaved on set (well, they would, I suppose). Mine had not. Peter the alpaca had taken an instant dislike to the presenters. Holly panicked and hid behind the sofa, as she is prone to doing, and Phillip received a face-full of alpaca spit. Luckily, the arrival of a vet who is familiar with the curious camelids quickly restored order.

After our respective scintillating appearances on the award-winning daytime show, we were both buzzing with the after-effects of adrenaline and chatted in front of the big screen where publicity photos are taken. Generally, this is the place for taking Instagram snaps, but we both found it hilarious and ridiculous in equal measure. At one point, Lorraine Kelly walked past, on her way to presenting her own award-winning show and said 'good morning' to both of us, just as if we were her best friends and it was completely normal to meet Graeme and Julian on a Thursday morning outside the green room. I've been in a few green rooms over recent years and, when talking about them, I always feel compelled to explain that they are not green at all. They are just like normal rooms and there is nothing green or special about them.

But that's fine, because there is no reason why these rooms

should be special. Because in fact, they are not filled with megastars or divas. Most of the time they are filled with normal people, doing pretty normal things, who just happen to be on telly. Like Graeme and me. Normal people, doing normal things but with interesting creatures as our subjects. This book explores a career working with amazing animals and it's an insight into Graeme's unlikely insertion into the world of telly. It's an interesting read and a journey with which I can entirely empathise. I hope you enjoy it.

Julian Norton, vet, Yorkshire Vet, author of vet books

Introduction

Introduction

If, 15 years ago, you had told me I'd be sitting down to begin writing a book about dogs, I'd have laughed: what I knew about dogs could have been written on the back of a postage stamp. After all, I was 40 before I even had a dog of my own.

It wasn't for the lack of wanting. As a boy, I – and my younger sister, Andrea – often asked our parents if we could have a pet. My mum and dad maintained it wouldn't be fair because we wouldn't be home enough. But there was something my dad used to say, which I realise now, after he's gone, had great significance: 'It's too upsetting when they go.' When I was older he told me a story from his childhood that explained perfectly why he felt this way. I've included it later, because this is a book of stories – the stories of dogs I've met and the people who love them.

I'll begin with my own. I grew up – dogless – in a market town in North Yorkshire called Selby. It was all right (which is Yorkshire-speak for very good indeed). I had a great childhood. My dad was an electrician in the sugar factory and my mum a swimming teacher at the local swimming baths, as was her mother before her. Later, I passed my Eleven Plus exam by the skin of my teeth and went off to school in Leeds, by train. It was a huge, great metropolis: it seemed to 11-year-old me that nobody in Selby had ever been further than Leeds or York.

The first dog I remember was a miniature, apricot-coloured poodle called Pepe, who moved into a bungalow opposite where we lived. He was quite a sweet thing. We'd ride around on our bikes and he'd always be there.

Funnily enough, the first dog I ever lived with was also a poodle. This one was called Noodle and he belonged to my pretend daughter, Apryl. (I've never liked the word 'step' when it comes to parenting, as in step-daughter. It seems to always go alongside 'wicked'.) Anyway, when I met Apryl's mum, Noodle the poodle was already a firm fixture and he and I got along fine.

In the years that followed, I came to know a couple of Rottweilers who were big lovable lumps. There's something very reassuring about a solid dog and I figured that if I was going to get a dog, I might as well go for the full-fat option. And so, a Rottweiler puppy called Axel entered my life, my first dog 'from scratch' (not one to do things by half – I got another one nine months later). There's something magical about having a dog from puppyhood. We went to visit the breeder three times before we picked Axel; the first time when he was just three weeks old. Later, when he was a great big 50kg powerpack of a boy, it amused me to tell people there was a time when I could hold him in one hand.

Having a puppy taught me that you've got to do things again and again and again. Because you teach them little things, like 'sit' or 'down' and you think they've got it, you might be inclined to assume, 'Great, that's that, then.' No, it's not, because tomorrow it seems as if they've forgotten and you have to tell them again. You've got to have patience and that's not something that came naturally to me.

I was working for Weetabix in Northamptonshire when I got Axel. I was an operations manager: I ran factories for a living. I came to it in an odd way, via a Hispanic Studies degree from the University of Hull. Weetabix was a long way from languages and dogs were a long way from Weetabix.

When I got the job in my final year at uni, and I announced it to my housemates, they all fell about, laughing. They all thought it was a joke because my diet mostly involved Weetabix – for breakfast, lunch and tea. I worked for the company for 21 years, starting off as a graduate trainee and then as a supervisor of about eight people making Alpen in a little factory in Corby. I worked my way up from there and, by the time I left, I was reporting to a company director and had about 200 people in my team.

* * *

It was Axel that got me into dog training. I'd already started to do the best job I possibly could with him because I've always believed that if a job is worth doing, it's worth doing well. So, this was my first time with a puppy and it was a pretty serious breed. Back in those days (in the early 2000s), Rottweilers were very much the media's designated 'evil breed'. The tabloid press just loved to show pictures of them baring their teeth. Whenever there was a dog attack, often involving completely different breeds, they'd roll out a stock picture of a Rottweiler and caption it with the cliché of 'devil dog'.

I was determined to be a responsible dog owner. I was also a serving special police officer at the time, so wanted to do the right thing and train Axel properly. I threw myself into learning as much as I possibly could. Then, nine months later, Gordon – the second Rottweiler – came along, and now I had not one but two of these great big dogs. It was a serious proposition.

I got involved in something called *Schutzhund*. It's German for 'protection dog'. In Germany, it's a tradition to train German shepherd dogs, but also other breeds, in the manner of police dogs, but only for trials and competitions. It's a civilian thing and the dogs are trained in obedience, in the way you often see at Crufts, as well as jumping over hurdles and up and down A-frames. Plus, they're trained in tracking a scent on the ground and protection work.

In learning about *Schutzhund*, I was learning about dog aggression and how to control it. And if you can learn the triggers that make a dog aggressive on command, as the police do, you're also going to know how to avoid it as well. You know how to turn it off.

The head trainer took me under his wing and every Sunday I spent every minute I could watching dog after dog come onto the training field, the trainer taking control and showing what to do, me trying to work out why on earth he'd done something different to the last dog.

I left Weetabix and was set on being a management consultant. I took three months off and, in this time, threw myself into the dog training. Towards the end, I told the head trainer I was off to be a management consultant.

'Why don't you be a dog trainer?' he asked.

'Why do you think I should do that?'

He then said something that changed the course of my life.

'Because you're good with people.'

'OK,' I said, a little surprised. 'What about dogs, then?'

'No, no,' he said, 'you're good with dogs, but there are lots of people who are good with dogs. You've got the dog thing and the people thing. You can do both and there's not many out there like that. So, I think you'll be very good at it. I think you should consider it.'

I jumped in my Land Rover and used the drive from Birmingham to Northampton to consider my future. (And when you drive a Defender along the slow lane of the M6, you've got plenty of time to think.) By the time I got home, I'd made up my mind. I was going to be a dog trainer.

I came up with a company name: The Dogfather, and put an ad in the local paper (the *Northampton Chronicle & Echo*) – the size of a postage stamp – and patiently waited by the phone. Nothing happened. I repeated the exercise the next week, and the one after that.

About a week later, at 8pm, the phone rang. It was a mobile number I didn't recognise. This was it.

'Is that the dog trainer?'

'Yes,' I replied, because that's what from that moment on I was.

* * *

When I went to see the person who had rung me a couple of days later, it was a dark November night in Northampton's Eastern District. We walked around as the dog pulled on the lead and we stopped under street lamps so I could explain things. I'd gone from a warm factory to a freezing cold pavement and it was hard work, but I was doing something I was growing to love.

Some advice I was given, from someone I really respected, before I started, was that it's not the letters after your name that matter most; it's the number of dogs that have been through your hands.

This was dog number one. There was a long road ahead.

The business built slowly. Initially, I didn't charge much: about £40 for a couple of hours' training. By the following March, I was holding Kennel Club-listed puppy and adult dog classes.

I would see more than 20 dogs, over three classes in an evening. If ever there was a hands-on intensive course in dog and owner behaviour, this was it. The business grew and I built a reputation locally and further afield. Within three years, I was working everywhere, from Scotland to the south coast of England.

During those years, when I'd done a really good job, I'd say jokingly: 'I should be on the telly, me.' I never thought for one moment it would happen and I never did anything to make it happen.

Then, one day, in 2016, eight years after I began, and totally out of the blue, the phone rang – like so many times before – and the caller said, 'Is that the dog trainer?'

But this was a different call altogether. It was a life-changing moment.

The woman on the other end of the phone was from a TV production company looking for a dog trainer to feature in a new show.

The premise was they wanted to follow me around the country helping dogs and their owners with problem behaviours (that's dog behaviour *and* owner behaviour!). From early on I was determined I wanted to be involved only if it were a show that could help dog owners and give useful tips and tricks of the trade, but also reflect how much fun dogs are.

I didn't think it would go anywhere, but happily went off to meet them. The more they talked about it, the more interesting the idea became. To cut a very long story short, we made a pilot which aired on Channel 4 before the show was eventually commissioned by Channel 5. As I write, we've just begun filming series three of *Dogs Behaving (Very) Badly*; after the 2020 lockdown, it's great to be out there again with the crew and, of course, meeting dog owners and their badly behaved pets.

It's a great show and I love working on it because it gives me the opportunity to help loads of people in one go. When I do a private, one-to-one consultation, it's me and whoever is at home; on TV, I can talk to more than a million people at a time, and many more on catch-up, too.

People often get in touch with the programme to say they've been following some advice given in a show and that it has helped fix their dog. It makes me happy – and proud – when that happens.

One of the most fun episodes was a celebrity special we filmed as part of a Channel 5 animal charity week. I got to work with Denise Van Outen and her gorgeous (if spoiled) French bulldog, Tilly; Michael Owen and his overly protective Staffordshire bull terrier, Ronnie; and opera singer Russell Watson and his nervous Saluki, Poppy. It was lovely to meet household names – on stage or on the pitch they're special, but at home they're real people with real dog problems, and it was a pleasure to help out.

I see this book an extension of that. It's a mixture of stories (a few of which *Dogs Behaving (Very) Badly* viewers will be familiar with) and a whole host of others that I've never told before. It's been, and continues to be, a huge learning experience. Into this book I've distilled more than a decade of knowledge gained not just from study but from many thousands of dogs and owners; however, the challenge has often been not what to put in, but what to leave out, so it's not exhaustive. In fact, I've found myself thinking many of these topics warrant a book in themselves (note to publisher, ha ha).

Although the stories are peppered with the science behind why dogs behave the way they do, this isn't intended to be a dull dog-training textbook. Instead, it's a collection of memories – often with a moral to the tale from which you'll learn lessons you can apply at home. I hope to leave you with a greater understanding of how to improve your dog's behaviour and – importantly – with the tools you'll need to interact in a way that works for you both.

I'm a heathen when it comes to reading books and don't necessarily start at the beginning or end at the end. Often I'll dip in, attracted by a particular chapter or word that jumps out at me – more like a posh box of chocolates than a packet of custard creams. I've split this book into two sections. The first covers off my guiding principles for improving dog behaviour. The second is about how this works in practice, with real stories that illustrate how to apply the principles with your own dog. You can read part two in any order you like, but it will make more sense if you've read part one, where, for the first time, I've detailed my Golden Rules for dog training (three and a half of them, to be precise). I'll explain how you can talk to dogs like I do – and understand what they are saying in return. I'll explain how you can time it like a pro, how to be a leader they'll willingly follow and why excitement might be at the root of all your problems. I've included some surprising scientific discoveries, too.

Recalling these stories has caused me to laugh out loud occasionally and also to shed one or two tears. That's because, as dog lovers know, to live with them is about heart as well as head.

I hope that in reading these stories, dog owners everywhere will come to understand their canine companions better.

Part One

Chapter 1
A lesson learned

June 2015

'You're not going home tonight. We need to get you straight to theatre.'

The A&E consultant was like someone out of a TV drama. Tall, good looking, his expensive shirt sleeves rolled up above his elbows and the purple shadows under his eyes suggesting the kind of tiredness that reaches your bones.

He was the fourth medic who'd looked at my hand and I'd seen the same expression pass over each of their faces as they referred me up their chain of command. Whatever was going on, it wasn't good.

'Can't you just stitch me up, give me some antibiotics and let me go home? I'll come back tomorrow.' I was not too hopeful of a positive response.

'Right now you can still feel and move those fingers,' he replied. 'That could change at any moment. We need to have a good look in there straight away, and assess the damage.' Clearly it wasn't negotiable.

* * *

This really wasn't how I'd seen the day going when I was munching my toast at breakfast. I had no reason to believe dog number 4,120 was going to be the one that made me think that perhaps, just possibly, I was not invincible. Not in my wildest dreams did I imagine this would be the day that – let's not mince words here – I'd be taken out by a German shepherd in ten seconds flat.

What follows is an account of a one-to-one dog consultation that became exceptional very quickly and for all the wrong reasons. It was my worst ever day as a dog trainer. It would have been easy to have left this story out of this book, but I decided not to. I learned important lessons from it and it may well be that you do, too.

Looking back, there were signs. I parked my car in front of my clients' house and immediately noticed the letterbox was missing from the white UPVC door. All evidence pointed towards it having been ripped out by a powerful dog; one who would literally do anything to get at the postman or, for that matter, anyone else who made it that far.

It was obvious Dave and Nikki, the friendly couple who welcomed me inside, were desperately out of their depth with the rescue dog they'd picked up just a week ago. We drank mugs of tea in the kitchen to the backdrop of the dog barking and snarling menacingly in the garden. He'd occasionally go silent as he hurled himself at the window just a metre behind me.

Nikki talked about the issues they'd been having and Dave apologised for the noise and general air of chaos. To be honest, the problem was so apparent I was having trouble concentrating on what they were saying.

Having listened to the catalogue of issues the couple were experiencing, from extreme aggression towards strangers to incessant barking, the obvious next step was to meet Zeus. The chest-tightening fear building inside me was hard to ignore, and this level of apprehension was unusual for me, but then again this level of aggression and in such a large dog was unusual, too.

I reminded myself I'd done this countless times and it had never gone wrong before. *Ignore the fear,* I told myself, *and press on*.

I asked Dave to bring Zeus in on a lead, explaining that this would give him control if his dog went for me. Dave was a reassuringly big lad.

The kitchen was small and, with the three of us and Zeus, there was little room for manoeuvre on the vinyl floor that, judging by the holes, the dog had already had a good go at.

'That lead is secure, isn't it?' I asked Dave.

'Yeah, don't worry, mate, he can't get loose.'

I asked Dave to allow the dog to get a bit closer and have a sniff of me.

Zeus lunged straight at my chest and I only just managed to step backwards out of the way.

'OK, Dave, that's enough. Bring him back to you.' I moved my hand a couple of inches – in the merest hint of a gesture – to emphasise the point.

Big, big mistake.

I've heard it said a dog can move their mouth four times faster than you can move your hand. I don't know if there's any science behind that, but I'm inclined to believe it. What happened next, I didn't see coming.

I knew I'd been bitten because I felt a massive clamping pressure, then a mighty tug. Zeus's teeth had pierced my left palm between the root of my ring finger and my little finger. The tug was Dave's perfectly mistimed panic reaction. He pulled Zeus off with everything he had, causing the dog's canine tooth to rip its way back out through the flesh of the side of my hand.

There was no pain – yet – and so what I saw seemed all the more surreal. My hand had been ripped open like a cut of meat in a butcher's shop window. I could see things moving only surgeons are meant to witness.

Blood began to ooze. Slowly at first, and then a little faster, like the slowest opening of a tap allowing a steady trickle of water to drip ... drip ... drip-drip into the sink. That drip became the thinnest of streams and, for the briefest moment, we all stood frozen, watching my blood form a crimson puddle on the vinyl flooring.

* * *

In A&E the enormity of what had happened – and what might have happened – began to sink in. The paracetamol wasn't cutting it and the pain was getting worse, both physical and emotional. I'd been stupid, a dog trainer whose schoolboy error had landed him in hospital.

Dave – who had driven me to hospital, ashen-faced and endlessly apologetic – popped his head around the cubicle wall. 'Are you all right, mate?'

'I've had better days, if I'm honest,' I replied, putting on my brave 'tis-but-a-scratch face. It was the understatement of the decade. There had been literally thousands of better days since I had decided to become a dog trainer. Right now I was wondering what had made it seem like a good career choice. Accountancy, quantity surveying or (God forbid) estate agency were all looking a much better bet.

* * *

It took a good few weeks to heal from the surgery but much longer to recover emotionally from the experience.

At the end of the day I decided to carry on, but told myself I needed to do things differently. I put new rules in place to avoid taking uncalculated risks in cases when aggression might be involved.

Getting bitten isn't big or clever. I've met dog trainers (male, all of them), who appear to see it as a badge of honour, as though running out of brains and skill confers bragging rights. Not in my book, it doesn't. And this is that book.

Chapter 2

Three and a Half Golden Rules

Have you ever wished you could get the dogs – and the people – in your life to behave better? If so, I've got a bit of good news for you: you absolutely can drive better behaviours and it's not complicated. All you need to do is consistently apply the simple rules I'll teach you in this book.

Many of us are fascinated by psychology, both dog and human, but all too often it's couched in technical jargon which can make it seem impenetrable. If you're anything like me, you really don't need impenetrable: you need simple, practical and effective rules to follow.

Canine psychology has a lot in common with its human equivalent; at least, it has much in common with the simpler aspects of human psychology. We are, of course, more complex than dogs – which may or may not be a good thing – but regardless of species we're all subject to some basic guiding principles that psychologists have known about for more than a hundred years.

Let me tell you about one of my favourite things. In 1905 an American called Edward L. Thorndike published a book called *The Elements of Psychology*, in which he proposed a theory of behaviour called the Law of Effect. Facsimile copies of his book are still offered for sale on the internet if you're interested, but here's a word of warning: unless you're a card-carrying psychology geek, you should only read it if you're suffering a particularly stubborn bout of insomnia.

More recent attempts at explaining the Law of Effect don't help the casual reader very much either. Take, for example, the following passage from Wikipedia. For a few years I've read it out loud, to comedy effect, when giving talks, because it's such a good example of the kind of impenetrable psychobabble I try to avoid when I'm training people (and the odd dog). Get your thinking cap on and try this for size: *The law of effect (. . .) states that when an S-R association is established in instrumental conditioning between the instrumental response and the contextual stimuli that are present, the response is reinforced, and the S-R association holds the sole responsibility for the occurrence of that behavior* [sic].

If I told you that 'S-R' stood for 'stimulus response', would it help? Probably not. Which is a great shame because in truth this little gem of knowledge is easy to understand when someone explains it in plain English.

Let me introduce you, then, to Graeme's Three and a Half Golden Rules. I follow them every time I work with dogs and their people. I've borrowed the first two from Thorndike. The third comes from somewhere else (I'll explain), and the half isn't so much a rule, as a not-so-obvious observation.

Graeme's Golden Rules

- Rule one: Any BEHAVIOUR that feels REWARDING will INCREASE
- Rule two: Any BEHAVIOUR that feels UNCOMFORTABLE will DECREASE
- Rule three: Some BEHAVIOURS that are IGNORED will FADE AWAY
- Rule three and a half: PRACTICE DOESN'T (ALWAYS) MAKE PERFECT

Let's look at this in more detail, starting with rule one, and break it down.

Rule one: Any BEHAVIOUR that feels REWARDING will INCREASE

There are three parts to rule one: Behaviour – Reward – Increase. Let's examine them one by one.

Behaviour refers to any action a dog takes, however subtle, whether it's desired (walking nicely on a lead, say) or undesired (pulling your arm off). When we think about rewarding behaviour, it's normal for us to imagine rewarding good behaviours – quite rightly. What's often missed is that bad behaviours are frequently rewarded by dog owners, too. They just don't realise they're doing it. You'll find many examples in this book of perfectly reasonable people doing understandable things that have the unfortunate effect of making their dog's behaviour problem much worse.

Some dogs are undoubtedly smarter than others. If you happen to have a clever one, you might want to think of their intelligence as a double-edged sword: your dog will learn the good things and the bad things equally quickly. Dogs are marvellously indiscriminate. If playing with a toy and pulling its stuffing out is good fun, they'll do it; if making a lunchtime snack of your fancy new sofa feels equally rewarding, they'll do that, too. To your dog, the size of the toy and whether it's 'good' or 'bad' doesn't matter. All behaviour is the same. That is, until you start to apply Graeme's Golden Rules to change how your dog thinks.

* * *

Reward What's the first thing that pops into your mind if I ask you to give your dog a reward? For many it's likely to be a food treat. There's nothing wrong with that for the right dog, at the right time, but the trouble with this approach is that it only covers one aspect of what is rewarding to your dog. It might be useful to reframe the way we think about this.

Let me suggest a new definition. A reward is ANYTHING that feels good.

It's simple as that. If it feels good, it's rewarding and that's enough to drive behaviour. The behaviour may not be desirable or wholesome – it could even be unsafe – but if it feels good to your dog, he's going to do it again and again, until something changes.

When you think about it, people aren't so different. Let's start with treats. I know custard creams don't form the basis of a healthy diet. Of course I do. I'm not daft and I know that I should just quit. Simple, right? But they're just *so* rewarding. I eat one (behaviour) and it feels good (reward), so I do it again. Ker-ching! The behaviour increases. Ker-ching! Ker-ching! Ker-ching! I'll quit tomorrow.

There are times when a biscuit simply won't cut it. (Hard to believe, right?) If I'm nervous or anxious to the point that adrenaline is kicking in, for example. Maybe I'm feeling fear tighten inside me – perhaps when a big dog is threatening to bite. Offering me a biscuit at that moment is almost certainly not going to get my attention. In the same way, if you have a nervous dog who is reactive on a walk, you may have noticed that pushing treats when he's wound up simply doesn't work. Even if you get your timing right, he'll likely spit out the treat if you force the issue. There are much better ways to help stressed-out dogs, which we'll look at later.

Although rewarding with food can work (for both dogs and their people), there are many other, sometimes better, ways to encourage a job well done. In the human world we often reward good behaviour with a kind word, a smile or a pat on the back, both literally and metaphorically. The truth is, this kind of attention works well with dogs, too. If a reward is 'anything that feels good', then praising with the right tone of voice, a smile (yes, they do understand our expressions) and a stroke or a cuddle can go a long way. Add treats and play into the equation and you've got quite a few tools in your box.

* * *

Increase When behaviours are rewarded, they increase in frequency, duration and/or intensity. So, for example, my biscuit habit. Here's the mechanism: driven by the short-term reward of a sweet and crunchy hit, I head to the cupboard more often; I practise my biscuit-disappearing trick for longer; and I go at it more voraciously than a starving Cookie Monster. I'm increasingly becoming a not-very-lean, mean, biscuit-eating machine. (The same applies to most Labradors with just about anything edible – and often quite a few things that aren't.)

Let's take a real-life doggy example. Diego was an unruly ten-month-old Rottweiler-Rhodesian ridgeback-cross I worked with during the filming of Channel 5's *Dogs Behaving (Very) Badly*. He was a lovely lad but incredibly boisterous, to the extent he frightened the life out of people with his antics outdoors. Diego had an unfortunate habit of biting people to make them play; he didn't mean to cause harm, but that was often the end result. Sooner or later, he seemed destined to be the subject of a dangerous-dog complaint, one which almost certainly would not end well for him – little dogs sometimes get away with misdemeanours like that, but sadly big black and tan dogs rarely do. As well as this worrying behaviour, he had a habit of barking and nipping for attention, at home. The fact was that his behaviour of running around, jumping at people, barking and ultimately biting to get attention had been getting steadily worse in the few months since the family had adopted him as a puppy.

I liked Diego as soon as I met him, but I imagined not everyone had this initial reaction to him. Although I've never had a ridgeback, I'd owned Rotties for years and I've long thought that to know one is to love one. Admittedly when it goes wrong with a Rottweiler, it can go very wrong and very quickly, but it is rare. Most of them are big, misunderstood teddy bears. What we had here, unless I'd royally misread everything, was a cuddle monster in scary clothing who had no idea whatsoever why people ran, screaming and flailing their arms around, when he bit them. What he did know – clever lad – was that it was the best fun ever when they did.

'Will he be OK?' asked a crew member, from behind his camera. We'd only been in the house for a minute. 'I mean . . .' He paused momentarily. 'What if he . . . err . . . what if he bites?'

In front of him, prowling tirelessly around the legs of each member of the crew like a black-and-tan tiger shark, was Diego.

'Oh, don't worry about him,' I said, reassuringly. 'He's a pussy cat. He's not going to bite you.' I paused to let the information sink in. What he was seeing, and what he was hearing from me, didn't quite match. 'Well, not a proper bite, anyway,' I added, somewhat less reassuringly. 'And if he does, I'll stop him somehow. It'll be all right.'

As risk assessments go, what I had said was a bit rubbish and I knew it sounded too casual.

'Okaaay.' He sounded less than convinced.

I needed to dig up a bit of gravitas, for everyone's sake. Of course I was taking it seriously – I hadn't taken my eyes off Diego in all the time that he'd been in the room – but it probably didn't seem that way.

'Let me explain exactly what to do if he gets lairy. OK?'

'Yes, great,' said the crew member.

'Well, basically, if he starts kicking off, barking, snarling, biting, all of that . . .'

'Yeah . . .?' He was concentrating as though his life depended on it. Probably because he believed it did.

'Don't move. Stay absolutely stock-still. Don't scream or shout. Do your best not to pull away, or his teeth will do more damage. Plus, your rapid movement will fuel the fire. That's a nightmare scenario. You really, really don't want to do that. Do nothing. Leave it to me and I'll deal with him.'

Silence.

I looked around the room at the rest of the crew. The sudden change in demeanour from my default of light-hearted humour to listen-very-carefully seriousness felt like dense storm clouds gathering on a summer's day: visceral, heavy and inescapable.

I allowed a few moments for everyone to process the information and broke the silence.

'There is one last thing,' I said. 'If he does start going bananas, and this is very important . . .' I paused for an indecently long time, a contagion of eager nods spreading around the crowded living room, '. . . whatever happens, for Christ's sake keep filming!'

I'm happy to report that no film crews were harmed in the production of the show and it all ended very well for Diego.

Let's consider how rule one applies in this extreme case: a behaviour (jumping and biting) is rewarded (people jump about and make sounds, providing the supercharged attention that Diego craves) and so the behaviour increases (it was becoming more intense and more frequent). A behaviour that had been rewarded, increased.

By applying rule one like a formula, it's possible to work backwards: if a behaviour that feels rewarding, increases, it follows that a behaviour that is increasing must be getting rewarded in some way. If you've got a dog-behaviour problem that is getting worse, ask yourself: how is my dog getting a kick from this? You're likely to find the answer is staring you in the face. Once you understand the reward a dog is getting from an undesirable behaviour, you're halfway to fixing the problem.

Rule two: Any BEHAVIOUR that feels UNCOMFORTABLE will DECREASE

Rule two is the opposite of rule one. Rule one stated that if it feels good, your dog will do more of it. The equivalent here is that if it feels bad, your dog will do less of it.

Let's break the definition down as we did for rule one:

Behaviour is any action, good or bad. As you may have guessed, we'll be using this rule mainly to reduce bad behaviour. However, perhaps surprisingly, we sometimes see the effect of it when an owner inadvertently sends the wrong signal at the wrong time and messes up good behaviour. Let's take an example.

This one is hypothetical, but it's something that often happens. You've probably seen it yourself many times.

A man – interestingly, it's rarely a woman who commits this particular misdemeanour – is in a field with his dog. Let's call the man Dick, and his trusty companion Spot, a liver and white springer spaniel. It's a beautiful mid-April day. The sun is high in a blue sky, streaked with cotton-wool wisps of white. Dick feels the warmth of its rays on his arms as he walks between the hedgerow and the fresh, green shoots of the farmer's crop. It's the first time this year Dick has ventured out in short sleeves and he's feeling rather pleased with his choice. It's been a long winter, but spring has most definitely sprung. A hundred metres away, Spot is enjoying himself, too. He's gambolling in the long grass, ears flailing with every bounce. He's excited to be rediscovering the thousand-and-one smells he'd almost forgotten existed. He's distracted, and happy.

'Spot! Here!' Dick's voice rings out in a bright and happy tone. So far, so good.

There's no doubt Spot can hear him – people over in the next village probably did – but Spot carries on reliving his puppyhood regardless.

'Spot!' Dick tries again, hardening his tone. 'Come here!' Spot stops and looks at his owner for a moment, any hint of puppy dog now gone, and then runs away, scared.

Dick snaps. Shouting and screaming at the top of his voice, his ego triggered by the wilful spaniel, he runs towards his dog but stops halfway to give it one last shot: 'WILL – YOU – COME – HERE!'

Finally, Spot freezes for three, perhaps four seconds, desperately trying to work out what to do next. Decision made, he starts a slow and foreboding return. His tail is locked underneath his body and with his head bowed, he's avoiding eye contact with his owner. Spot has seen this happen before and knows it's a no-win situation. If he doesn't go back, he'll get told off, but if he goes back ...

Within striking range of the man now, Spot's fears come true. 'Bloody dog!' Dick shouts and, before Spot has a chance to flinch, the stunning blow of a time-honoured tap to the nose is dealt.

To an animal with such a sensitive nose, the effect is more than uncomfortable. It's out-and-out painful. 'Bad boy!' Dick adds for good measure.

Quite apart from the inappropriate way Dick told off his

dog, there's an issue here about timing. If a recall has failed, it's failed. There's no point telling a dog off after the event. Instead, we should think about going back to basics and retraining a quicker and happier response. Our hypothetical Dick made things even worse for himself and his dog: he punished poor Spot precisely when he came back.

Poor old Spot was stuck in a dilemma. If he didn't go back, he'd be a 'bad boy', but then he'd also be a 'bad boy' if he did. For him it's a lose/lose situation. He's confused, scared and unhappy. Ironically, he's also less likely to come back in future.

There's all kinds of wrong that's happened here: there's no reward for good behaviour; Dick's method of telling off Spot was way over the top; and his timing was spectacularly bad to boot. Spot didn't stand a chance.

For decades, psychologists have known that purely negative feedback is a very inefficient way of training a person or an animal, quite apart from the moral questions it raises. Experience tells us that nagging has some effect, but it's limited. I know I've never responded well to it myself. I tend to push back when people nag. Perhaps you do too, and I've seen that in dogs, many times.

While there's definitely a time and a place for the purely positive approach, it's absolutely clear that purely negative is never the way to go. I once met a man who spent his time going around advising dog owners that they should never, ever show any affection to their dogs because it was a sign of weakness and their dogs would think less of them for it. The only thing they understood, he preached, was punishment because, 'That's what learns 'em.' I was inclined to disagree, but I did learn from him, nonetheless. I learned how not to do things.

It's pretty obvious when you think about it. Telling a dog repeatedly what you don't want him to do, without actually telling him what you DO want – and rewarding that good behaviour – makes no sense at all.

Back to Dick. As well as not praising good behaviour, the other thing he did wrong was to overdo the correction, ultimately because he let his negative emotions get the better of him. The end result was deeply unpleasant for Spot.

There is a real risk the bond between dog and owner is irrevocably damaged in situations like this. Bullying a dog into submission is not the way it should be. As much as I'm all about training dogs to get results for the people who pay me to do so, I'd rather see a naughty but happy dog than a compliant one that is demoralised, confused or frightened.

* * *

Uncomfortable You'd be forgiven for thinking that what I'm saying here is that all forms of correction are bad and we should never tell our dogs off. In fact, I don't subscribe to that view. It's OK say no – literally or otherwise – but it's a question of degree, and too harsh a correction is much worse than none at all.

So, what's the level of correction we're aiming for?

Uncomfortable is just that: it's not a euphemism for 'beat them up, shout at them and make them feel scared until they comply'. With any negative consequence, your aim should be to use the lowest level that will have the right effect. If you can look at your dog in a disparaging way and it does the trick, well, good for you. You don't need to – and shouldn't – go further.

To explain what I mean by uncomfortable, let's take a real-life example. Some years ago, I moved to an area in the country where my main route to pretty much anywhere involved a quiet A-road where the authorities, God bless them, had placed not one but two fixed speed-cameras on a dead-straight road. In a quiet modern car, travelling at the 50mph limit felt like standing still. Nonetheless, being as law-abiding as the next fellow, I always stuck to the limit. That's not to say (and I'm not condoning this) that on occasions my mind didn't wander, and my speed crept up. Every time it did, though, I'd feel very uncomfortable and roll off the accelerator until I was well under the limit. Those cameras take no prisoners.

Over a period of around three years, I reckon I've been past the two cameras over a thousand times. That's a thousand mini training exercises, concentrating on getting the speed right because not doing so brought the threat of a letter arriving in the post with an invitation: give money to Her Majesty's government and collect a few points on your licence, or go and have your day in court. Either way, that's uncomfortable. It's not physically painful or psychologically scarring, but it is an uncomfortable feeling, and one, I reasoned, that was well worth trying to avoid.

So, one day, there I was barrelling along the road after a long hard day's work, mentally singing along with Adele on the stereo and fast approaching – not that I'd thought about it yet – the first of the infamous speed cameras. At the last moment, but without enough time to brake, my conscious brain kicked in. 'Oh, hell!' I blurted out aloud, involuntarily shooting a quick glance down to the speedo. The awful truth was . . . not so awful: 50mph. Not 51, nor 49, but 50mph exactly. Hallelujah!

That was lucky, you might say, but in fact luck had very little to do with it. By consciously modifying my behaviour to avoid an uncomfortable feeling, I'd created a habit. While my conscious mind was mid-duet with Adele on stage at the NEC, my subconscious had taken over control of the eyes-brain-right-foot-on-the-throttle-pedal loop that sets the speed. It was a remarkable result.

My autopilot had engaged purely to avoid discomfort. At no point was I rewarded for exhibiting the good behaviour that Warwickshire Police were after: no smiling, happy policeman ever popped out from behind the bushes to stop me, no boxes of Milk Tray were proffered to express the chief constable's eternal gratitude. Not even a kind word or a patronising pat on the head because I'd been a 49mph good boy. Not a sausage. (Which, if I were a dog, wouldn't do at all, of course.)

The fact is that, although we might not like to admit it, speed cameras do change the way we drive. Not by rewarding good behaviour, but by making unwanted behaviour feel uncomfortable. It's a rare example of a system where, even with supposedly intelligent animals such as humans, avoidance of uncomfortable feelings creates behaviour change, slowly but surely.

* * *

Decrease You might be forgiven for thinking a behaviour that's decreasing is easy enough to define. If we're talking about barking, for example, clearly a decrease means less barking. Not necessarily no barking, but less. Sometimes we'll get lucky and eliminate the problem altogether, but it rarely happens overnight. Less manifests itself in different ways, and each one is a sign you're on the right track.

Here are three telltale signs of a decrease. We might see a behaviour becoming:

- Less frequent
- Less intense
- Shorter in duration

Take the example of a dog that's barking at other dogs on a walk and apply the criteria above. For our purposes here, it doesn't matter why he's barking – whether he's shouting, 'Come here! I want to play with you!' or 'Get away from me, I'm scared of you' – if we're assessing improvement as we train him to be calmer, I'm looking to see if there's a trend toward less frequent barking, less intense barking, or barking that lasts for less time. Let's look at each in turn.

Less frequent: If your dog previously barked at every dog he saw, is he now barking at fewer dogs? If he barked at dogs and people, has he given up on people, even if he's still barking at dogs? If the problem is intermittent, how long has it been since he last did it? Have we moved from: 'He embarrasses us on every single walk' to, 'He's not perfect, but we've had three great walks so far this week'?

Less intense: Listen to the barking. In the same way a person's tone of voice can tell us about their emotional state, so it is with a dog's bark. You may hear the bark change from: 'I absolutely WILL get what I want and I jolly well know it' to,

'I'm still barking but I don't really know why any more. This isn't working and I'm thinking of giving up.'

Shorter duration: There are times, for whatever reason, when a dog's behaviour doesn't appear to improve at all in terms of either frequency or intensity, but if you pay attention you'll find he's not keeping it up for quite so long. It can be a subtle thing, but it's there and is a sign that things are beginning to improve. Perhaps we have a dog that used to bark until another dog was completely out of sight, even if that was the other side of a playing field. Now he stops barking at half distance. It's easy to miss these telltale moments unless you're looking out for them; instead, we tend to focus on what's wrong. In fact these shorter-duration indicators are a good sign the tide is beginning to turn. Unfortunately, it's also the very point at which many frustrated owners give up, thinking it's not working. Sadly, they'll never know how close they were to a breakthrough.

* * *

With over-excited dogs, there's an important variation on the theme of shorter duration – the time it takes them to calm down after the trigger that caused the excitement has gone away. Whether the trigger is a dog in the park, a parcel-delivery guy knocking on the door, or your neighbour's taunting cat parading along the back fence (cats do that on purpose, right . . . ?), try to assess if they're calming down more quickly.

There are absolutely times when an unwanted behaviour is as frequent and intense as ever, and your dog is keeping it up for as long as the trigger is present. To all intents and purposes, you may say there's no improvement. Unless, that is, you take note of what happens afterwards. It's not uncommon for the first signs of change to be a dog that calms down more quickly.

Everything is relative, and a question I often ask in the middle of a training session is: 'How does this compare to normal?' The responses vary from, 'About the same,' to, 'He's like a different dog.' Either way, the answer is always useful.

It's a question you should ask, too, if you're training your dog, because it's important to be clear where you are starting from. So jot down notes on the problem before you begin. How intense is it? How frequently does your dog do it? For how long does he keep it up – both during and after an event?

Having a clearly defined start point is the only way to know how far you've come.

Rule three: Some BEHAVIOURS that are IGNORED will FADE AWAY

There's a place for ignoring some unwanted behaviours in the hope they will diminish. Choose the right time and you're on a winner; ignore the wrong things, though, and you could make the problem worse. To help understand when to ignore bad behaviour and why, let's break down the definition:

'Some behaviours' – you'll notice that for rule three, I've chosen to say 'some behaviours' and not 'any behaviours'. This is because there are behaviours which should not – cannot, even – be ignored, and others that could be ignored, but doing so won't help you or your dog.

The mantra of rewarding good behaviour and ignoring everything else is limited by practical considerations. In cases of aggression, for example, it may well be dangerous to ignore unwanted behaviour: we simply cannot shout across to a person being mauled by our dog in the park: 'He'll stop eventually.'

Even dogs that are being friendly but are scaring people unintentionally shouldn't be ignored. My Rottweiler, Axel, a beautiful big teddy bear of a dog, was fascinated by small children in buggies: given half a chance he'd be in there, nose first, checking them out, purely because he was inquisitive. To let him carry on would have been crazy. Axel was young at a time when the UK tabloid press was referring to the breed as 'devil dogs', and the moniker stuck. For his own benefit I chose not to ignore Axel's habit.

There are times when it's entirely possible to ignore something a dog is doing wrong, but it won't help you to improve the problem. In fact, ignoring it might allow it to get worse. Take, for example, the classic problem of a dog that barks at the postman. Here's the sequence of events: Postman Pat walks up the garden path and Killer the Pomeranian barks his little head off. The post, nevertheless, is delivered. Killer is still frantically cursing and swearing as Pat turns on his heel and runs away (actually, he doesn't run away at all, but as far as our misguided Pom-Pom is concerned, he might as well be Usain Bolt). Killer, not entirely unreasonably, comes to the conclusion that defending the house (behaviour) feels good (reward) because of the magically disappearing Royal Mail employee and therefore he'll do it again tomorrow. And again, the day after that.

If we could speak with Killer directly in Pomeranian language, we might explain he'd jumped to the wrong conclusion. We'd explain post-people are good and that they go to every house bringing nice things (we'll gloss over the bills). We'd say Pat didn't run away – he was always going to leave, regardless of whether or not Killer barked. The barking was just a coincidence.

Killer simply wouldn't agree. He'd see it in very black-and-white doggy terms: 'I think you'll find I barked,' he'd say. 'And the nasty man went away. What part of that don't you understand?'

So, we could ignore Killer's barking until the cows come home, but it wouldn't make any difference. On the contrary; while we're doing nothing and he's taking matters into his own paws, our pint-sized protection dog is rewarded by the sight of Postman Pat beating a hasty retreat every day. The end result is that ignoring Killer will most likely allow his barking to become worse. Unless of course, we kidnap the postie and chain him to the front gate until Killer gives up on the barking. Do that every day for a couple of months and Bob's your postman (because Pat resigned weeks ago). It's probably illegal, though, and definitely not a nice thing to do. So please don't.

In effect, the problem we have is that his long-suffering owners can't stop Killer from being rewarded by his barking. That's unfortunate, because any form of reward creates increased behaviour. What's needed is an effective and humane way of making the unwanted behaviour uncomfortable.

There are, however, plenty of other behaviour problems where owners are in full control of the reward. Broadly speaking, most attention-seeking problems fall into this category. When it comes to attention seeking, ignoring the behaviour may well be your best option, provided you know the rules. Let's take a look at that.

The psychology we're employing when we ignore something is called behaviour extinction. When a behaviour doesn't produce a desired result, it begins to fade away, to become extinct, but only if it's met by the same brick wall lack of response each and every time.

Attention-seeking behaviour has to be ignored completely in order to work. This is an all-or-nothing strategy. Ignore something even most of the time, but give in occasionally, and it won't work because each time your dog gets what he wants, you'll be right back to square one. Worse still, he'll quickly figure out that you don't mean what you say, and it's worth pushing his luck even more. A double whammy. Ignoring a naughty dog is often easier said than done, but for it to work there can be no chinks in your armour. Set out your zero-tolerance stall before you start and, if you don't think you can keep it up, choose a different technique.

It's also important to be aware that once you start the ignoring process, your dog's behaviour may get worse before it gets better. It's a phenomenon psychologists call the extinction burst and you'll see it clearly as a peak on the graph overleaf where diminishing behaviour is measured over a time. It is counter-intuitive that behaviour should become worse in the early stages and not better, but that's exactly what happens in many cases and it's important to know this in advance.

Incidentally, if your dog gives up – even for a few seconds – and offers a better behaviour instead, I would always reward this to create more of it. If this seems familiar it's because we

Figure I

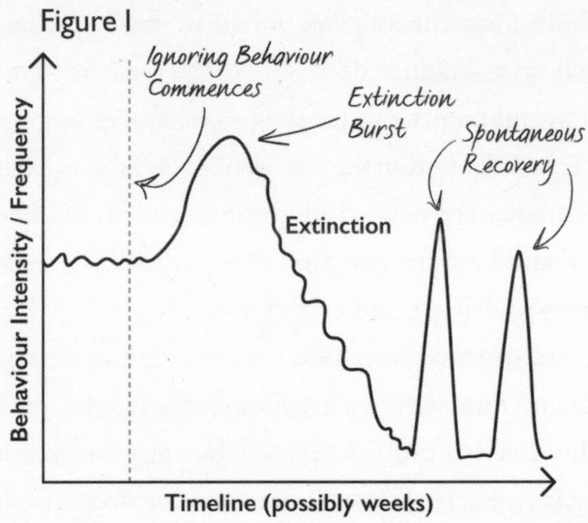

talked about it in rule one. The message is clear: do this (bad behaviour) and you'll fall off my radar. I'll ignore you. But do that (good behaviour) instead, and I'll give you the attention you're craving. It's a clear choice and, if there's one thing dogs like, it's clarity.

* * *

I've come to think of behaviour extinction in the context of the psychology of knocking your head against a brick wall. It's a process that takes a long time. I'm sure most of us have, at some point in life, had a moment of realisation that whatever we're doing is a waste of time and effort. It's a familiar feeling, but what's really interesting is that, at the point we realise that what we're doing is futile, we don't stop doing it. In fact, we typically carry on, ignoring any and all evidence to the contrary, in the hope something will change.

Eventually, we lose enthusiasm until finally we admit defeat and stop. Even then, however, we may go back and try again because, well, you never know. It's not so much a lightbulb moment followed by an immediate change of approach, as a gradual downhill progression, often interrupted by moments of thinking, 'I'm just going to give this one last shot, and throw everything at it.' Those last-shot moments are collectively referred to as 'spontaneous recovery' and I am referring to them in the plural because – contrary to what we sometimes tell ourselves – there are usually two or three 'last' shots.

Dogs and humans are very similar in the way we progress through behaviour extinction (and many other aspects of dog psychology, too). That's useful because if we have been there ourselves, we are well on the way to understanding what a dog is thinking.

Spontaneous recovery last shots don't happen every time, but it's so important to be aware of them because it's often the point at which the whole behaviour improvement strategy goes crashing off the rails. The spikes in the graph are short in duration, but of extremely high intensity and so, when a dog appears to revert to their original bad behaviour, it's not surprising that this is when many owners throw in the towel.

Helen and Paul, an older couple I went to see, lived in Surbiton with their five-year-old yellow Labrador, Judy.

'We named her after Judy Garland,' explained Paul. 'I can't remember how it came about, to be honest, but it seemed a nice name and there was this little jokey thing that we used to do. When she was little, I used to drive her up to Richmond Park for a walk and we'd trot along with me singing, "We're off to see the wizard, the Wonderful Wizard of Oz" . . . she used to love that.'

I smiled. The idea of a mild-mannered retired accountant from Surrey skipping down an imaginary yellow brick road in the park was incongruous, but entirely believable. Dogs bring out the best in good people.

I looked at Judy. She was sitting on her bed next to the fireplace, seeming very much like a permanent fixture. She had greeted me at the door an hour earlier with a whole-body tail wag before waddling off into the living room of the seventies executive des-res where she'd lain down on her bed and hadn't moved since.

She was a mellow lump of a dog, covered in soft, shaggy sandy fur. To meet her was to love her. And there was a lot of Judy to love.

'She likes her food, then?' I said, more statement than question. I had insider knowledge. 'My assistant, Sarah, made lots of notes for me. She told me Judy often pesters you for food. Does it work?' I smiled and raised an enquiring eyebrow.

Paul cracked into a laugh. 'Ha ha, yes, you could say that. You know, we try to ignore her when she does it but she just barks and barks until she gets fed. She'd keep it up for ever if you let her. She's very persistent.'

'When you say that you try to ignore her, do you mean you ignore her for a bit and then you basically fail to ignore her?' I offered a cheeky grin to take the sting out of the question.

'Well, yeah, I do, I must admit. But it's really hard.'

'It is,' I conceded. 'You're absolutely right. Anyone who thinks ignoring a dog is easy has never had a hungry Labrador!'

Some Labradors have a mutated gene, which sheds some light on their tendency to seem constantly hungry. The gene concerned, known as POMC, regulates how the brain recognises hunger and, in particular, the feeling of being full after a meal. In a 2016 study, researchers at Cambridge University's Wellcome Trust Medical Research Council Institute of Metabolic Science looked at 310 pet and assistance-dog Labradors and discovered that almost a quarter (23 per cent) had this genetic defect and, as a result, were an average of 1.9kg heavier.

In effect, it is likely that the affected dogs quite literally never know when to stop eating. For many Labrador owners, this won't come as much of a shock, particularly as the study also found many of the cohort without the POMC gene variation were still motivated by food. So, starting with a breed that's food-motivated at the best of times, take away the 'I feel full' mechanism and it's no surprise some Labradors pester for food. Little beggars.

It's not all bad news, though. Interestingly, assistance dogs were discovered to be slightly more likely to have the genetic variation. That makes sense because using food rewards to train a dog that is constantly hungry makes for a good chance of success (and a happy working dog). But imagine how awful it must be to feel hungry all the time, never able to switch off the feeling.

Incidentally, if you thought you were off the hook because your Labrador's weight gain is genetically hard-wired into her brain, think again. Despite her best efforts, she's not in control of how much food she's given; that responsibility lies with you.

In Judy's case, we'll never know whether or not she fell into the unlucky 23 per cent, but she certainly acted as though it were a matter of life or death whenever her people prepared food for themselves.

'She's calm enough now,' Paul remarked, 'but as soon as we sit at the table to eat, she barks her head off. Goodness knows what the neighbours think.'

To prove the point, we moved to the G Plan teak dining table with matching chairs and Helen brought out a home-made Victoria sponge – all in the interests of science, you understand. There are perks to my job – not only would it be rude not to eat the cake, but it would be remiss of me not to experience Judy's party trick first-hand.

Sure enough, Judy struck up a deep, resonant chorus as soon as the cake came out.

'Uff! Uff-Uff!'

'Does she . . .'

'Uff!'

'Does she, er . . . does she always . . .?'

'Uff! Uff!'

'Does she always do this?' I shouted, between barks.

It was a question I probably needn't have asked because the answer was written all over Helen and Paul's exasperated faces as they nodded in unison. They were clearly used to mealtime gesturing with guests. Shouting over the din was a waste of time. Helen waved a pointy finger, alternating between the cake, my plate and back again, nodding and smiling in the universal sign language for, 'Help yourself.' She was clearly fluent. Years of practice.

'Uff! Uff! Uff!'

Judy's barking was not showing signs of abating. If anything, it was getting worse. It was as though she were protesting that even though I was the new boy, I was being fed cake and she wasn't. How very dare they!

As soon as we'd had our tea and cake, we went back to the sitting room to chat. Judy stopped barking as soon as the plates had been removed to the kitchen.

'How does the barking normally end?' I asked.

'Well,' Paul explained, 'sometimes we give her a chew-bone to keep her distracted while we eat, but that's about the only thing that works. We've tried telling her off – that doesn't work, or at least not for long – and we've tried ignoring it, but she's just so wilful. She keeps on and on.'

I was curious because this was just the sort of attention-seeking behaviour that should, theoretically at least, respond well to behaviour extinction – if it's done properly. 'Tell me more about ignoring it, Paul. Has it ever worked?'

'Ah, well, that's interesting.' Paul became more animated, shuffling forward on his seat to make the point. 'Yes and no. We had a behaviourist lady out about a year ago and she told us to ignore it and it would stop. We had to completely blank the dog – no eye contact and definitely no titbits – and stick to our guns. God, it was hard work, but we did exactly as she said.'

He was right, this was interesting. Why hadn't it worked?

'Didn't it work at all, then?' I asked

'No. Load of rubbish. We put loads of effort in and it got worse, if anything. £200 down the Swannee.'

I was no closer to understanding why the ignoring strategy had made Judy worse, but then Helen chipped in.

'No, darling, that's not quite right. It got worse to start with, remember, but afterwards it did improve for a while.'

'Not for long.' Paul crossed his arms in defiance. 'We did everything we were supposed to. We really did completely ignore her while she was barking and I think we got about six weeks out of it. But then she started barking again, as badly as ever. It came from nowhere and she's been like it ever since. Waste of money.'

'Hang on,' I said. The penny had dropped. Between them, they had just described a classic case of extinction burst followed by some success and then – by the sound of it – spontaneous recovery. 'So, let me get this straight. You started to completely ignore her and the behaviour got worse initially, as though she was trying harder, not taking "no" for an answer?'

'Yes, that's it,' Paul confirmed. 'I was a bit surprised, to be honest, but I thought we should persevere and, Helen's right, Judy did start to get better. I'd forgotten that. She started to bark less. Or at least, when she did bark, it was very half-hearted.'

'She pretty much gave up altogether, Paul, before it stopped working,' Helen added.

Perfect. This was beginning to sound like a textbook example.

'So, what went wrong?' It was the obvious question.

'One day we sat down to dinner and she started barking again. For the life of me, I can't think why it happened. It was just a normal night, but for whatever reason she fired up and the barking was every bit as bad as ever. As though someone had flicked a switch. She started barking again and she's been like it ever since.'

'OK,' I said. 'I think I know exactly what's happened here. Can I just check something? What did you do next?' I felt sure he must have rewarded it. Almost certainly without realising it, but I'd bet my bottom dollar on it.

'Well, I was frustrated, you know. All that money and weeks of ignoring her. And just when we seemed to have cracked it . . . Well, I told her off. That didn't work and then I suppose I ended up reasoning with her. You know, "Come on, be a good girl and you can have your dinner afterwards." I know I must sound crazy, negotiating with a dog, but I didn't know what I was supposed to do. So, in the end, I thought I'd distract her and . . . oh God . . .'

He slumped back in the sofa and paused for a moment. 'I've just realised what I did. I thought I was distracting her because I got a big chewy bone thing from the kitchen to keep her quiet.' He paused. 'I rewarded the barking, didn't I?'

'Yes, you did,' I replied. 'It's understandable. You're not the first and you won't be the last. But it was the wrong thing to do at precisely the wrong time, I'm afraid.'

'But she completely reverted. Honestly, she went straight back to square one. Surely just rewarding the barking once wouldn't do that, would it?'

It was a perfectly reasonable point; after all, it does sound unlikely that she'd revert so completely. But that's not allowing for the spontaneous recovery effect. Just as Judy was at the peak of her bad behaviour, she hit the jackpot and made an obvious connection. *Barking does still work, but only if I try really, really hard*. Dogs can be surprisingly smart where food is concerned.

This was a case of so close and yet so far. What Paul and

Helen didn't know – could not have known at the time – was that they were at the peak of a very short-duration last shot on Judy's part. It was a critical moment, a fork in the road. If they had persisted with ignoring her, there was every chance she would have given up within a day or two. What happened was typical of a pattern I see frequently: dog lulls owners into a false sense of security and then reverts to the bad behaviour, giving it everything she's got and . . . bingo! Her owners give in. But who can blame them? And who can blame the dog for carrying on barking?

All of this sounds like the worst sales pitch ever for ignoring unwanted behaviour, except for one thing. There are times when telling a dog off simply isn't possible and ignoring them is the only way. Take a dog whining for attention at night, as an example. If you go down to her and tell her to be a good girl, you've rewarded her. If you go and tell her off, she may, if she were anxious, become scared of you, particularly if you over-do it through frustration. And if you tell her off but she was attention seeking, then she got the attention she wanted. All attention is good attention, for a dog.

Judy had no issues with anxiety. Her owners followed my advice to the letter and happily it worked, the barking is no longer a problem. If there has been a change in behaviour in *your* dog and they seem anxious, it's important to understand the root cause, and so it might be a good idea to seek professional help.

Behaviour extinction affects people and dogs alike. We follow a similar pattern: I'm not giving up straight away; I'm going to try harder because this has always worked (extinction burst), followed by the same gradual knocking-head-against-brick-wall decline (extinction) and, if you're unlucky, the same last shot (spontaneous recovery) phase. Ignored behaviour fades away over a long timescale that's more often measured in weeks or months, rather than hours or days.

So, there it is: ignoring behaviour sounds easy, but it's not. Whether you're reading this book as an owner looking for solutions or as a dog trainer, don't let me discourage you from using behaviour extinction, but do be aware of the pitfalls. Forewarned is forearmed.

And the half: Practice DOESN'T (ALWAYS) make perfect

Humans are impatient animals. We expect instant results – probably more so now than ever in these days of instant messaging and same-day deliveries. We get frustrated when things don't go our way quickly. Becoming aware of small improvements helps a lot. When people see me working with a dog, it's not unusual for them to remark that I'm a patient man. 'Tell my mother that,' I always reply. 'She'd fall over laughing.'

In truth, I'm not very patient at all, but when I see incremental improvements in a dog's behaviour I'm getting feedback all the time. Most people don't notice these small changes, but when you've worked with dogs for years it becomes second nature.

Intermittent problems are particularly difficult for us to cope with emotionally. When you've got an issue that comes and goes – or when a dog reacts to certain people and not others, or some people sometimes, but not all the time – the tendency is to see everything in negative terms. For sure, it's frustrating and owners are often on edge, just waiting for the bad thing to happen. That's understandable, but it's also very pessimistic.

The focus is on the fact that the dog is sometimes bad. If you turn that on its head, the focus is on the fact that he is sometimes good. Glass half full or glass half empty? By definition, this is always true in a case of intermittent behaviour: unfortunately, we almost always hone in on the bad stuff. The inevitable good moments go sailing by unnoticed, and often unrewarded. This is a huge missed opportunity because a behaviour that's rewarded increases.

I had a call from a client I had seen two weeks previously. She was the owner of Tilley, a Border collie who was reactive to strangers. Tilley would strain at the lead, snarl and bare her teeth at anyone who passed by. I had not heard from the lady since the one-to-one consultation and I had rather assumed things must be going well. Certainly, we'd had a great result on the day.

'Graeme, I'm having a terrible time with Tilley. I've had a complete disaster. She's just gone for someone on a walk!'

'Blimey, I'm sorry to hear that,' I said. My heart was sinking and a thousand and one questions were flying around my head. I asked Tilley's owner to talk me through exactly what happened. Sure enough, Tilley's behaviour sounded almost as bad as when I had first met her and – worse still – my client, who was herself a little highly strung, sounded distraught. It's remarkable how often our dogs mirror us. I've seen it many times.

'She seemed so good when I was there,' I ventured. 'When did things start to go wrong again?'

'Oh, yes, she was. Really good. And she's been loads better

ever since, to be honest, apart from today.' Before I could interject, she added an afterthought. 'She was fine on the rest of the walk before it happened, too.'

'OK,' I said, 'so, let me get this straight. She's been a good girl for two weeks. Is that right?'

'Yes, she really has.'

'OK. So how long was today's walk, before it all kicked off?'

'Oh, about an hour. It happened in the last five minutes, just before we got home. Just when I thought I'd cracked it, she ruined it.'

'Right, let's put this into perspective,' I suggested. 'Without wanting to downplay the bad behaviour today, she's been good for two weeks and today it was only the five minutes at the end when she was bad. Really bad, I get that, but two weeks and 55 minutes of "good girl" followed by five minutes of bad isn't really a *complete* disaster, is it? Even though I know it feels that way.'

It's one of those things that instantly becomes obvious as soon as you hear it but, naturally, it's not obvious when you're looking through the pea soup fog of emotion. Intermittent problems are exhausting, but when looked at logically they're usually nowhere near as bad as they seem.

Tilley had messed up. There was no doubt about it. It was also true we had taken a step back in her training. But it wasn't a disaster by any means, even if it had seemed that way at the beginning. We all learn from our mistakes – at least we do if they are pointed out to us in the right way – and dogs do, too.

Humans tend to make the same mistakes repeatedly. Anyone who ever learned to drive in a manual car will have graunched the gears more than a few times before they finally got the hang of it. It's more than simply being able to change gear smoothly when we really concentrate. We end up in a position where a smooth gear change becomes second nature and we can hold a conversation or wonder what's on the telly tonight as we're doing it. Dog training is like learning to drive. It takes practice, and you can't expect your learner to get it all in one lesson.

There is a phenomenon known as one-shot learning, which is fairly self-explanatory. The textbook example of one-shot learning is a toddler putting their hand into a fire. They only do it once and learn quickly and permanently not to do it again. The obvious downside to one-shot learning is that the level of stimulus required to create quick learning is extreme, usually involving a high degree of pain or fear. It's also, by its very nature, purely negative. There's no place in modern dog training for it, but I mention it purely to illustrate that if we're training without pain or fear, it follows that we'll have to repeat things a lot.

Practice is something that I used to do a lot when I was into ballroom dancing, and it's from the world of dancing that I've borrowed rule three-and-a-half. To keep me and my dance partner, Lin, on the right track, we had a lesson most weeks with a brilliant teacher called Gary Foster. He was a top-flight professional dancer (and now a respected competition judge). He knows dancing inside out, never misses a trick and his scalpel-sharp sense of humour makes him a very easy chap to like. This means he can be very blunt at times without causing offence.

We had finished dancing a foxtrot and done quite well at it, so we moved onto a quickstep. It had never been our best dance, but I thought it was going reasonably well until I danced past Gary. I could see out of the corner of my eye that he looked perplexed. Clearly it wasn't going quite as swimmingly as I had thought. He stopped the music. 'Well, your foxtrot was good,' he said, with a wry grin. 'I'll give you that!' The lowest form of wit it may have been, but it was funny and it made the point.

Experience told him that something wasn't quite right and that something was probably me. 'Graeme,' he said, 'dance the third line on your own for me, would you?' I knew I was in trouble. It's hard for a judge to see exactly what is wrong sometimes when a couple dance together, but he had been in this business since Fred Astaire was a lad.

I danced my best dance and the judge's verdict was in: 'Lin, you're off the hook.'

Turning back to me, Gary had a question. 'Tell me the names of the figures you're supposed to be dancing.'

'Yes, sure,' I said. I knew this one. 'Scatter chassé, scatter chassé, scatter chassé, double lockstep, then a quick open reverse.'

Gary cut in. 'Spot on.' I'd got something right, then. 'And what are your feet meant to be doing on the double lockstep?'

I knew that one too: 'Toe-toe-toe-toe-heel, isn't it?'

'Correct.' I felt the warm glow of smugness creeping over me, but I knew Gary well. There was no way – not a snowball's chance in hell – that this was about proving how clever I was.

Sure enough, a smile erupted on his face and he suppressed a chuckle. 'The only problem is that that's not what your feet are doing. You're dropping two heels in at the end. Toe-toe-toe-heel-heel. Try again!'

I danced it again, being sure – or so I thought – to follow the prescribed format.

'No! You've done it again!' Gary shouted over the manic beat of Sinatra's 'Jeepers Creepers'.

'Did I? Are you sure? I could have sworn I did it right,' I shouted back. I wanted to believe my instinct, but I knew there was no way Eagle-Eyes was wrong.

He said nothing because his smile said 'we both know I'm right'.

We did.

And so it went on, dancing it again and again until we were sure that my feet were indeed talking to my brain. It was a good spot on Gary's part and I was grateful.

'Right,' I said. 'I'll make sure I've nailed it by next week. Practice makes perfect and all that.'

'No, it doesn't,' he replied, quick as a shot. 'Practice doesn't make perfect.'

Had I heard that right? How could practice not make perfect? Surely everyone knows that practice makes perfect.

'Not in your case, it doesn't,' he added.

What kind of a riddle was this?

'Practice,' he pronounced, triumphant, 'makes *permanent*. And if you're practising the wrong thing – whether it's dancing or dog training – it's not going to be perfect, is it?'

There is no point arguing with Gary Foster. He was, as ever, quite right. Practice makes perfect only if you're practising the right thing. The principle applies equally well to dogs, dancers and learner drivers.

So, while practice might not make perfect, enough practice will make habits – both good and bad – permanent.

Train the wrong way, and the chances are you'll be making things worse.

* * *

My Three and a Half Golden Rules are the cornerstones of good behaviour. There's a lot of building still to do once the foundations are in place, but a solid base is the best place to start. If you're ever getting confused or frustrated with your dog's behaviour, bring yourself back to the basics. In every case, the following apply:

- Rule one: Any BEHAVIOUR that feels REWARDING will INCREASE
- Rule two: Any BEHAVIOUR that feels UNCOMFORTABLE will DECREASE
- Rule three: Some BEHAVIOURS that are IGNORED will FADE AWAY
- Rule three-and-a-half: PRACTICE DOESN'T (ALWAYS) make PERFECT

Put another way: when you respond to your dog's behaviour, the way it feels to your dog will fall into one of three categories:

- Feels GOOD
- Feels BAD (uncomfortable)
- Feels like nothing

There really are no other possibilities. How you respond, and how it feels to your dog, drives changes in behaviour – both good and bad. To a large extent, you and those around you have control. Possibly more than you realised.

Chapter 3
How to talk to dogs

'This dog hates me, mate. Don't get me wrong, I've never laid a finger on him, but he won't come near me. I don't know what I've done to get his back up, but he hates me. That's all there is to it.'

I'd come to the East End of London to see a family whose American bulldog-cross was pulling badly on the lead. Bread and butter stuff for me, even if the dog concerned was an especially big boy.

Dodge was a massive 70kg and none of it flab. No one knew what he was crossed with, but whatever it was it had given him a head as big as a grizzly bear and a naturally powerful physique. His smooth coat – all brindly Bournville with patches of Milky Bar white – had a polished sheen that showed off his musculature and bore testament to the real care and attention he was getting. Someone was obviously looking after him.

He was named after the all-American Dodge Ram truck: six litres of roaring V8 power in a huge double-cab pick-up twice the size of a Land Rover (and about half as useful – did

I mention I like Land Rovers?). There were no two ways about it: this dog was beautiful. Beautiful and well loved.

Something, though, wasn't quite stacking up. He wasn't a rescue dog, for a start. There was no: 'We don't know what happened to him before we got him to make him like this'. No: 'He was abused as a puppy by a large man with a cockney accent.' Nothing. No clue whatsoever as to why he might hate this man.

Ron was quite the imposing V8 character himself. There was nothing soft about this guy's appearance. The five o'clock shadow on his shaven head betrayed a receding hairline and a hard, bony skull. His eyes were dark and deep set and a flattened, crooked nose hinted at a few 'interesting' nights on the town (I wasn't about to ask). At 50-odd, his physique wasn't quite rippling muscle any longer but under the middle-age padding was a heavyweight you wouldn't mess with. He sat holding court on an old carver chair. The wood was painted red and was scuffed, exposing the oak underneath. Leaning forward, legs wide apart, work-booted feet flat on the floor, his forearms rested on the tops of his thighs and his ham-like hands were clasped together. If he bumped into you accidentally in a pub and splashed your London Pride down your cravat and waistcoat, you'd be inclined to apologise quickly and buy him a replacement pint. And yet, the *Lock, Stock and Two Smoking Barrels* daydream over, the reality was that, despite the Ray Winstone-meets-Vinnie Jones demeanour, he seemed a really nice guy.

He gave me a cup of tea and sat me down in the only other carver chair. I was honoured, or at least I made a point of looking suitably honoured. My Yorkshire market town upbringing hadn't prepared me for the finer points of East End etiquette. I felt a bit out of my depth.

Ron explained that he hoped I could help him because his whole family loved Dodge – even if Dodge didn't exactly love him. 'Everybody judges a book by the cover with Dodge,' he said, 'but – no word of a lie – he's lovely. A gentle giant is what he is, mate, especially with my little granddaughter.'

Dodge wasn't the only gentle giant in the room. It's funny how you end up like your dog, isn't it? Ron bent forward and held a pleading, outstretched hand towards his dog. Dodge was lying near me with his chin on the floor, looking away from Ron.

'Come here, Dodgey boy.' Nothing. Not even the merest flicker of recognition.

It would have been impressive if the dog had been trained to stay and steadfastly to ignore a command like that (most dogs famously never sit still when you point a camera at them, for example). Dodge wasn't being fabulously obedient at all, of course. Quite the opposite. He was doing the doggy equivalent of waving two fingers resolutely in the air. And no one, I figured, flicked two fingers up at Ron.

'So, why's he hate me?' Ron's tone of voice betrayed a don't-tell-the-geezers-down-the-pub secret: he was hurt. When it came to Dodge at least, he was as soft as butcher's tripe. Here was a man, sitting in front of a dog, asking that dog to love him.

There was no way in the world he'd ever hurt Dodge. What was going on? In truth, I had no idea.

'I'll be honest,' I said. 'I don't know yet. I believe you when you say you haven't hurt him. I know it's not that, but there will be a reason. There always is. Always. Dogs don't lie. I want to understand this before we go out for a walk because, although I can show you lots of techniques for lead walking, the truth is that if he's looking at you thinking that you hate him or whatever's going on, it's simply not going to work.'

I needed to get into Dodge's head. I glanced at my watch. It's a telltale bad habit of mine, a reflex action that gives away what I'm thinking: *This is going to take a while – so much for my quick and easy bread-and-butter job.*

The house was a Victorian terrace with all the style giveaways of an eighties makeover. There was a bay window at the front and the room went back a long way. What was originally the sitting room had been knocked through decades ago to the back room and it was possible to see from the street to the garden. It made for a long tunnel of a room and I was sitting in the middle of it, perched on my wooden throne next to Dodge's man-sized crate. To my left was a small dining table, pushed up against a woodchip magnolia wall, with Ron sitting sideways on, facing me.

'Thing is,' Ron continued, 'I'm the only one in the house who can tell him off. If anybody else tries, he thinks they're havin' a laugh and carries on doing whatever he's doing. Not that he actually stops for me for very long, which is where you come in.'

'That's interesting,' I said. 'So you think he hates you, but he does at least have respect for you? Tell me more.'

'He loves Debs. Follows her around everywhere like a puppy. She can't even go to the toilet on her own without him tailing behind. Doesn't he, love?' Ron turned to look at his wife, sitting on the sofa behind me to my right.

I hate being in the middle at the best of times, doing my best tennis-umpire impression as people speak, looking left or right when each new point is made; I much prefer to be on the end of the table or seated in the chair in a corner with a full view of the room. I can see everyone and every dog at the same time. That way I can read the body language around me, dog and human alike. It's surprising what you pick up when you listen with your eyes.

Debs, who was tiny in comparison to Ron, was sitting on a pastel blue leather sofa, her legs, clad in faded, tight denim jeans, tucked under her. Her long, blonde hair was pulled back in a high ponytail and she wore a baggy pink jumper and comedy fluffy piggy slippers. (Am I the only one who thinks novelty animal slippers are a bit odd? They make it appear the animals in question befell an unfortunate accident, whereby in an incredible twist of fate not one but two human feet became lodged up their backsides.)

'He loves his mummy,' said Debs, in a bright and happy tone, while making the kind of coochy-coo face grown-ups pull when playing with babies. 'Don't 'cha, Dodgey-boy?'

Right on cue, Dodge stood up from where he'd been at my feet and bounced over to her and was given a cuddle for his trouble. I might have been new and interesting, but I was clearly no match for his mum.

'He loves you, doesn't he?' I said to Debs, putting to the back of my mind that Ron probably wouldn't approve of my assessment of the situation. 'Can I ask you a question? Do you think you baby him a bit?'

'A bit . . . ?' Ron's voice, now behind me as I'd turned to talk to Debs, hammered through. 'More than a bit.' I didn't respond; instead, I smiled and nodded encouragement to Debs, still facing her. It was her turn to speak.

'Oh, yes, he's a proper mummy's boy,' she said, ruffling up Dodge's cheeks with both hands and grinning like the Cheshire Cat. I wouldn't have thanked her for it, but the dog – as if to prove the point – was loving the attention, half-closing his eyes and tilting up his head for more.

'Who's a good boy?' Debs cooed in a lilting, almost musical tone that suggested delight more than pride. Funny how most women seem delighted with good dogs and most men seem mainly proud of them.

'OK, so if you stand up and pretend to pop to the loo,' I said, 'what will he do? Would you mind?'

'OK, sure. He'll follow me. He always does. And then he'll be a pain in the neck outside the door.'

I pointed into the hallway where there was a downstairs cloakroom. 'Go on, then. Let's see what happens.'

'What, now?' she asked, not unreasonably.

'Yes, please. I realise this has nothing to do with lead walking but humour me. I just need to see how he behaves.'

I was intrigued as to why Dodge would be so anti-Dad and so pro-Mum. There had to be a cause. There's always a reason that dogs do what they do, even if sometimes we humans can't quite see it. They both seemed perfectly lovely in their very different ways. Had I got that wrong? I think I'm usually a pretty good judge of character. Or perhaps I was right after all, and it was Dodge who'd got the wrong end of the stick.

Debs got up and walked to the loo. Dodge, right on cue, followed like an overgrown puppy dog. He looked up as he walked, as if to say, 'Where are we going, Mum?' He was an optimist; I'd give him that.

The door closed behind her with a clunk and a sign hanging on a hook on the outside rapped out its rhythmic message: Live, love, laugh. *Tap, tap, tap*.

Then nothing. Quiet. But not for long. Dodge had other ideas. He must have seen his mum go to the loo a million times. A million times she went into the funny little room; a million times she came out. If she went in, she came out. In. Out. Simple as that. There was nothing to worry about. And yet here he was, crying and whining away as though he'd never see her ever again. Softly, almost inaudibly at first, but then building to a crescendo, full-fat 'Nessun Dorma' by baritone dog. And very impressive it was too. Not quite the full Andrea Bocelli, but not at all bad. Then again, he'd clearly practised it a few times. It was impressive and irritating in equal measure.

'Dodge. Pack it in!' Ron's voice thundered out from three feet behind my left ear. The effect on Dodge and, for that matter, me, was quite literally stunning. I flinched, ducking down in my chair momentarily and then, feeling like a prat, pretended I hadn't.

'*Boom. Boom, boom, boom!*' is what Dodge will have heard, and it stopped him dead in his tracks. The reaction was instant, but ultimately temporary. Dodge started up again until, in mid-aria, with the squeak-scrape of a door handle and the single clack of an inspirational quote hitting plywood, the door opened.

Job done. I could almost see Dodge's brain working. *The louder you yodel, the quicker she comes back.* It's not over until the big dog sings.

'Don't do that, darling. It's naughty.' Debs's voice from behind the door was soft and lovely, pleading almost. 'Come on then, be a good boy,' she said, as she reappeared from the loo, bending down to stroke Dodge.

He'd got what he wanted – and crying was the trick that got it for him. A behaviour always increases when it is rewarded. The door opening and Mum reappearing, with a tone of voice that suggested praise more than telling-off, will do it every time. Although he clearly didn't like being told off by Dad, by all accounts it was worth suffering it in order to bring Mum back.

The contrast with Ron's approach couldn't have been more obvious. They were poles apart: Ron's booming don't-mess-with-me tone; Debs's audible strokes of lilting 'Mummy loves you' softness.

The funny thing was they could learn a lot from each other. Debs needed Ron's firmness when it came telling off Dodge, and Ron needed tones more akin to Debs's softer voice when praising him.

I ran back through my mind what I'd just heard. From Ron, 'Pack it in!' sounded like, '*Boom ba-boom*.' It was a perfect telling-off voice, and the reason he was the only one in the household Dodge listened to. So far so good, then. What didn't make sense was the way he was attempting to praise Dodge: 'Good lad.' That still would have sounded like '*Boom boom*' to doggy ears – the same tone as his telling-off. Ron might as well have been shouting 'Bad boy!' as the sound was the same. No wonder Dodge thought his dad hated him, poor lad: Ron did nothing but tell him off, or at least that's the way it sounded. Dogs can be quite clever at learning keywords – commands/requests – but they're pretty rubbish at understanding whole sentences. They rely much more on the sound of what we're saying to decipher what we're trying to tell them.

It's certainly possible to teach dogs many words if you have lot of spare time, patience and expertise: more than a thousand words, in fact. A study published in the journal *Behavioural Processes* in 2011 showed that a Border collie named Chaser learned and retained the proper nouns for a huge number of objects. Chaser's owner, John W. Pilley, retired emeritus professor of psychology at Wofford College in South Carolina, was given eight-week-old Chaser as a gift from his wife, Sally, and began teaching the puppy to recognise words for her different toys.

Chaser proved to be so adept that Professor Pilley made it his mission to find out quite how many words she could learn. More than three years later, he completed his research paper and the results were incontrovertible: Chaser understood 1,022 words. Clever girl.

Chaser's story is impressive, especially considering most pets I meet understand fewer than 20 commands. How does Chaser compare to the average person? Little humans learn very quickly. A 2017 report published in *Applied Psycholinguistics* journal found that one-year-old children recognise around 50 words; three-year-olds, typically 1,000 words; and by the age of five, children recognise at least 10,000 words. To find out how many words adults understand, in 2016

Ghent University's Department of Experimental Psychology used a social media questionnaire which prompted a million responses.

The average American native speaker of English, it turns out, has a vocabulary of 42,000 words by the time they are 20. This rises to 48,000 by the age of 60. That's around 50 times more words than the smartest dog ever tested.

So, if words aren't the most important means of communication, what about tone of voice? For years, I've been convinced of the importance of getting this just right. Experience told me it worked, but evidence was hard to come by until scientists had the bright idea of training dogs through positive reinforcement to lie stock-still in an fMRI scanner long enough for experts to see how the dogs' brains reacted when they were played different sounds. fMRI scans detect what's happening in real time within the brain, whereas conventional MRI scanners simply show static images. In an fMRI, when certain areas of a brain are active, the image on the screen shows these regions lighting up in bright colours. It's the difference between showing what a brain looks like and how it's operating.

By comparing fMRI scans of dogs and humans listening to the same sounds, biologists at the Comparative Ethology Research Group in Budapest, led by Attila Andics, PhD, established that human and dog brains look remarkably similar in terms of which parts of the brain operate when processing sounds. In a fascinating study, scientists played dog and human sounds with varying emotional associations, such as crying, laughter, whining and play-with-me barking, to both groups. Unsurprisingly, perhaps, the dogs tended to respond more obviously to dog sounds, while the people tested were more reactive to human voices. What was groundbreaking, however, was clear evidence that a dog's brain absolutely recognises the difference between negative and positive tones of voice (or 'emotional valence', in psychology-speak).

For me, the conclusion is clear: your dog understands the tone of your voice. It's hard-wired into the circuitry of their brain. Sure, you can teach them words and many of those can undoubtedly be useful; if you're skilled, have three years to spare and you start with the right puppy, you might even teach 1,000 words. Alternatively, you can make sure you get your tone of voice exactly right and you'll see results today.

Meanwhile, in the East End, poor old Dodge was struggling to understand his humans. All he had to go on was tone of voice. And, frankly, Ron and Debs weren't helping him very much.

If he could speak, he'd probably have told me: 'See? I whine and he tells me off, then I'm quiet and he tells me off. How crazy is that, right? I'm confused. Humans are weird.' It was hardly any wonder he didn't stop the whining for long.

This was quite a turn of events. In the red corner was a man whose every doggy communication was negative, but on my right, in the blue corner, was a woman who conveyed delight and contentment in her voice 100 per cent of the time. Even when she shouldn't. Her lovey-dovey, 'Good boy!' was delightful – rightly so – but the problem was her, 'Don't do that, darling,' was even more delightful.

Here was Dodge's thinking: 'If I'm a good boy, she praises me. If I sing she loves me even more. She adores me and she never tells me off. Unlike meany-pants over there.' As far as Dodge was concerned, Ron always told him off and never praised him. Debs always praised him and never told him off.

It's one of those things that, once you realise it, instantly becomes obvious. So obvious that I couldn't believe I hadn't realised what was going on until I saw it in action.

Understanding what's wrong is only the start, though; putting it right is something else entirely. The key to fixing the relationship was to get Ron and Debs using the right tone of voice at the right time. There would be occasions when Ron would need to sound a little like his wife to create praise, and other moments when Debs would need a little of his East End gravitas to pull off an admonishment.

I thought I would begin with Debs. It seemed it might be easier. I already had the right image in mind for her.

'We need to find your "Don't mess with me" voice,' I told her. 'Your praise voice is fine. So, don't change a thing there. It's your telling-off voice I'm worried about. Can I ask a slightly odd question?' This query always piques interest and the answer is always the same.

Debs looked quizzical, but said, 'Yes, of course.'

'When you were a teenager,' I asked, 'did you ever do something really bad that crossed the line with your mother?'

It's a rare person who answers no to that.

'God, yeah. Loads of times.'

'What was your mum like when she caught you out? In particular, what did she sound like?'

Debs crossed her arms, tilted her head to one side and rolled her eyes. 'You wouldn't mess with my mother, honestly. She can still be quite scary now and she's 83. She'd be, like,

"YOU, young lady, are in BIG trouble," and that was that. I'd be grounded.'

It was as if Debs turned into her mother as she spoke, growing two inches in her seat, her back straightening and her face turning to ice-cold granite.

'And were you like that with your own kids?' I asked.

'I suppose so,' she conceded. 'I'm not as tough as my mum, but they don't mess me around. They know when I mean business. I was always on it with the kids, but Dodge gets away with murder.'

That was music to my ears. 'So, if you need to conjure up the right tone of voice for telling-off . . . ?'

'I just need to be like my mum.'

Perfect, I thought.

For my next trick I just needed to get Ron to channel his inner girl. I was going to need all my people skills if I was going to pull this rabbit out of the hat. I explained the reasons why Dodge was reacting in such very different ways towards each of them, imitating – as respectfully as I could – their very different tones of voice.

'So, Ron, in order for Dodge to understand that you're praising him, I need you to adopt a new, softer tone of voice. Right?'

Ron was, to say the least, unsure. He threw himself back into his chair, half turned his head away, squinted slightly and – raising an incredulous, bushy eyebrow – said, 'How do you mean exactly?'

'Well, essentially, when you're praising him, you need to sound like Debs.' As soon as the words came out of my mouth I knew I was in trouble.

'Sound like ... Debs?' He repeated the offending phrase. His reaction was unambiguous. 'NO.' It rang out like the boom of a kettledrum.

'Sorry?' I was playing for time.

'No, mate. It ain't happening.' I was grateful for the 'mate', but struggling to see a chink in the armour to negotiate. If I couldn't fix the way he had been communicating, I would be sunk before I started.

I remembered he'd mentioned his granddaughter. I asked more about her. Olivia was 18 months old, the daughter of the couple's eldest son and a hugely smiley, happy baby. Ron clearly doted on her. I was onto a winner.

'Do you mind me asking what sound you make when you're soothing her off to sleep?'

'Well, I'm kinda like: "Good girl. Sweet dreams."' He stretched the words, calmed them down. The volume of his voice was lower; the tone was perfect, a deep amber honey. Smooth, viscous and sweet. It sounded totally natural and not at all forced.

'That's it!' I said, clicking my fingers. 'That's the sound. It's lovely. Perfect for praising calm behaviour. Just do that. You don't need to sound like Debs. Forget I even said that. Just sound like you do when you're being a granddad. OK?'

Ron looked enlightened. 'I can do that, mate, yeah. No problem. So let me get this straight. For telling off, it's, "PACK IT IN" and for praise' – in a heartbeat, his face changed from geezer to granddad – '... it's kinda "Good boy. Good boy Dodgey."' He smiled at his dog. 'Is that right?'

I held off answering. There are times when I can tell a dog is about to do something special and this was one of them.

Dodge was stretched out on the rug in front of Debs, in the way dogs do after a long nap. He was looking unerringly at Ron. *Come on Dodge, do it,* I thought, willing him with everything I'd got. Dodge got up, sniffed in Ron's direction and slowly walked over. He nudged his head up under Ron's forearm, asking for a cuddle.

'He doesn't hate you now, does he?'

'Mate, he's never done this, never.' Ron looked bemused, emotional and grateful as he stroked Dodge's head.

For a short time we all just enjoyed the moment. 'Ron,' I said, breaking the silence, 'you thought he hated you, but in truth he never did. At the same time, he thought you hated him. That wasn't true either. It's just been a huge misunderstanding caused by the wrong tone of voice.'

Sometimes, we change one small thing and the effect is massive.

'But before we go resting on our laurels, we've got a dog to walk.' I reached for my jacket. 'Shall we go and get his lead?'

Chapter 4
Touch is a powerful thing

I had a conversation with an expert canine massage therapist a few years ago. I wanted to understand a bit more about this kind of therapy and if it might be helpful with behavioural issues. It turns out it can be, particularly in cases of what I call 'bear with a sore head' syndrome. This is when a dog's bad behaviour is caused or exacerbated by underlying pain. The therapist said something that I thought was great: 'Hugs are drugs – and your dog is an addict.'

'That's brilliant,' I said. 'If I ever write a book I'll borrow that. Don't worry,' I added, 'I'll say who I nicked it from.'

Except, I now have a little problem: many moons have lapsed since then and I cannot, for the life of me, remember the lady's name. If perchance it was you, please do let me know because I owe you a drink! (Enter stage left: 326 canine massage therapists, all holding a hand in the air.)

Most dogs love appropriate physical contact. Appropriate because trying to hug a dog you don't know or even giving a face-to-face hug with a dog you do, isn't advisable. We can rev dogs up with touch or we can reward nice behaviour with a smoothing of the fur. The trick is to match the right touch to the behaviour you're trying to create – calm or excited.

For calm, read slow. In the same way that a slow, calm voice has a different effect to a rapid-fire staccato one, so it's the same with touch. For example, if you need to let your dog know he's being a good boy because he's not barking, use a long, slow stroke – take twice as long with every pass as you normally would – or a gentle tickle on his chest. Keep it light and lovely.

For a police-dog handler holding back Muncher the Malinois on the training field before she lets him loose, lovely is not the first thing on her mind. There's a time for excitement and this is it. She'll be patting and ruffling him up, revving him up to the high heavens before she unleashes him to take down the nasty man in the padded suit. She doesn't want Muncher to lick him to death.

That said, generally the problem isn't that we're too calm when we're trying to get dogs to behave themselves. It's the opposite. We use touch to excite them when we probably shouldn't. And we don't even know we're doing it.

Take my dad, for example. Every time I took my Rottweilers up to see my parents, the dogs were always excited to be there. They were young and full of enthusiasm for the world. Despite my fledgling dog trainer best efforts to keep them calm, every time the back door was opened, 100kg of hairy hurricane flew in, sending furniture and elderly parents tumbling like skittles.

It's hard to keep two young, crazy-happy boys calm when your near 80-year-old dad is crazy-happy himself and whipping up a whirlwind with shouts of, 'Hello, Axel!' (to Gordon, invariably – it was a 50-50 shot, but he managed to get it wrong every time) and 'Hello, Gordon!'

While all this was going on, my mum would do her best to stay out of the way, watching out for her antique mahogany whatnot with its precious cargo of delicate china. At times, it seemed not so much damage limitation as damage observation.

If the random excited greetings weren't enough (they would have been – thanks, Dad), he had another trick up his sleeve: as the boys bombed about like two steel balls in a pinball machine, he'd pat them on the side of the chest whenever they were in reach. These weren't gentle, calming strokes, oh no: they were full-on, open-handed, friendly wallops, resounding like kettledrum beats. Good lad! *Thump*. Come on! *Thump*. Calm down now, *thump-thump*. Off they'd go again at a hundred miles an hour, bouncing off furniture until they eventually ran out of puff and Dad, too, got tired of the thumping game. 'By go! They're lively!' he'd announce, as he collapsed contentedly back in his armchair.

Yorkshiremen can be prone to understatement. By the time he'd stopped winding them up, they weren't lively, they were hard-wired to the moon. The problem – if you can call it that – was that he loved dogs. He'd loved them since he was a boy, growing up in a pub in the market town where I was born, but in a very different time.

Dad's early teenage years ran parallel with the war. Times were uncertain and Dad's heroes were the RAF bomber crews who drank in his parents' pub, the aptly named Volunteers' Arms. Crews came and went. Sometimes they were posted to another airfield, other times their absence was unexpected and final. From time to time, Dad would ask after a pilot or crewman he'd become friendly with and the boys – for they were barely older than him – would simply say, 'He won't be coming back, Johnny.'

The one constant in his life was an Alsatian. For many years, the term German shepherd was frowned upon. During the war, and for decades afterwards, dog lovers preferred to think of them not as German at all, but Alsatian, from across the border in Alsace. The dog's name is lost now in the mists of time and sadly it's too late to ask the question, but Dad clearly doted on him and, I imagine, played the thumping game with him, too. One day the dog was re-homed. I don't know why. I rather fancy he may have eaten one of the pub regulars and was deemed bad for business, but Dad never said.

I wonder if, even after half a century, the memory was simply too raw. The dog with no name was taken to a new home near Leeds, 15 miles away. Within a week he'd found his own way back and waited on the pub doorstep for my dad, only to be removed again. One more lost friend, never to return.

When I was growing up and asked about a pet dog, there was sensible talk of 'big responsibilities' and how 'having pets ties you down.' The comment that always stuck with me came from my dad: 'It's just too upsetting when they go.'

From the time he lost his wartime companion, Dad never did have another dog. No wonder he was crazy-excited when the canine grandsons came to play. I see fewer men and big dogs playing the friendly thumping game these days; it's slowly given way to a frenzied kind of stroking and ruffing-up of fur. That's OK because, whether we want it or not, things move on. It's the way of the world. Axel and Gordon have gone now, bless them. My dad, too. All three went just 15 months apart. *Thump . . . Thump . . . Thump . . .*

It's just too upsetting when they go.

Chapter 5

How dogs communicate

What sound do dogs make?

If 'bark' or 'howl' or any variation on the theme popped into your head, go and stand in the corner and pick up a pointy hat.

Only joking. How about if I asked, what sound do dogs make for 80–90 per cent of the time? You'd have got it. Dogs are a lot quieter than we realise. Even when there's a nuisance barking problem, it's almost never such a high percentage of the time as it feels because we focus on the problem, the barking, and not the quiet moments.

Incidentally, if your first thought was indeed dogs are mostly silent, then congratulations: pick up a gold star and go to the top of the class.

We think this way because humans are naturally verbal. Although we know perfectly well that communication can be non-verbal, in order to make ourselves understood, we default to talking. It's what we do. Unless we're in a lift or on the Tube, of course, in which case God help you if you say hello to anyone.

Even if dogs aren't 'talking' as much as us, it doesn't mean they aren't communicating, because they lay great store by body language. That's not to say it's their only way of interacting – far from it – but never has the adage that seeing is believing been truer than with dogs. We'd do well to bear it in mind when we're with them.

For many years, I've been following a succession of scientific studies from universities around the world. Generations of academics have attempted to explain how dogs understand people and to what extent they can recognise not only our facial expressions, but also connect them to emotions.

At a very simple level, if we smile, we're happy and if we frown, we're unhappy.

Although it's tempting to think it's obvious that dogs understand our emotions – and certainly people since time immemorial have sworn their pets know how they feel – it's only since technologies such as eye tracking could be applied that we've been able to say for sure that it is true – to some extent – and explain why. There have also been a few surprises along the way.

An article published in 2015 in the journal *Current Biology* reported on a study from the University of Veterinary Medicine in Vienna, Austria. The article was entitled 'Dogs Can Discriminate Emotional Expressions of Human Faces'. Researchers trained dogs to nudge a touchscreen image with their noses when they saw a smiling person. If they chose the happy person instead of an angry-looking person, they would automatically be rewarded with a treat. The success rate was high.

At this stage, all that could be established was that suitably pre-trained dogs could indeed tell the difference between facial expression in humans. It was a big deal, but it didn't prove that dogs understood what lay behind the expressions, that smiles were indeed good and scowling was bad. There were, however, some big clues along the way.

For a start, it became obvious in training that some dogs showed a natural reluctance to nudge the angry face on the touchscreen, as though (surprise, surprise, you may say), they already knew instinctively that getting in the face of an angry person wasn't a clever thing to do.

In further studies, eye-tracking technology has shown researchers precisely where on a screen dogs are looking. Although we can't ask dogs what they are thinking, the eyes are a window into the brain. Knowing exactly where they are scanning is an indication of what is going on in their heads. The first thing to note was that, like humans, dogs focus on the human eyes and mouth to figure out what expressions mean.

The big surprise was that dogs do something which had only previously been seen in humans and other primates – they scan the left side of a person's face as they see it, first and foremost (i.e. the person's right side). It's a neat trick, called left gaze bias, which saves time in not processing data because faces are, to a large extent, symmetrical. More significantly, perhaps, when humans scan the left side of someone's face, the information is processed in the right hemisphere of our brains, where facial and emotional recognition takes place. The inference is that dogs may be instinctively using left gaze bias to understand our facial expressions both quickly and accurately. Clever dogs.

Furthermore, in studies where the response time was compared between humans and dogs, there was a strong indication dogs make up their minds more quickly about the people they meet. If you've ever known a dog to take an instant dislike to someone and be proven right, you've probably thought: 'My dog knew the man was a wrong 'un. I should have listened to him.' Well, now you know why.

At least possibly you do, because it could be that dogs are more easily distracted, or there's another reason they look for less time before making up their minds. But given that they came from a wild ancestor who would have needed to make very quick decisions about whether or not another animal was friend, foe or dinner, it makes sense they developed the ability to judge things rapidly. On the other hand, researchers also postulated that we humans spend longer looking at other human faces because we're processing more information, such as sex and attractiveness. If it's true, then the fact is not only can your dog read faces but he's actually quicker at it that than you are.

A 2016 study at the University of Lincoln in England, reported in the Royal Society journal *Biology Letters,* showed dogs combine both what they hear with what they see to come to a conclusion about a person. In the same way we know to expect a happy sound from a smiling person, and vice versa with an angry-looking one, for the first time it has been shown that another species can do the same.

The study of dogs continues and, for the first time in a follow-up study by the University of Lincoln, reported in the journal *Animal Cognition* in 2020, the instinctive behaviour of dogs who had not been pre-trained was assessed by eye tracking. The researchers also compared how humans view dog expressions. The results showed that the way in which our eyes scan a face for clues about the emotions of the subject (gaze patterns) is hard-wired into our brains. Most of us know what expressions mean in our own species. And here's the catch: humans are wired for humans and dogs for dogs.

I was interested to read that, compared to dogs, humans spend only a fraction of the time looking at dogs' ears. Perhaps in the way we think it's all in the eyes, dogs would tell us it's in the ears instead. Even more fascinating is that dogs watch our noses when we are fearful. If there was ever any doubt that dogs understand our expressions, think about this. When we're scared, our nostrils dilate slightly, almost imperceptibly. It's so subtle that we hardly ever pick up on it. (Cor! Look at the nose on that bloke, he's terrified! said no one, ever.) We might not process it, but according to the studies, dogs absolutely do.

It's food for thought, isn't it? What I've always taken from this is that we need to bring our body language into play when we're communicating with dogs. If you're pleased with them and you want to encourage more good behaviour, look happy! You'd be surprised how many people don't.

Equally, if you want your dog to believe you when you're telling them off, you need a facial expression that matches. It's why, if you've ever seen me on the telly, I'll be frowning one minute but smiling like a Cheshire Cat the next. I'm sending out signals.

It's unusual for us to create a complete mismatch (happy voice and frowning face, for example) although I have come across it. A flat and expressionless face is more common, especially when we're concentrating. The unfortunate coincidence here is that when people are focused on getting their dog-training technique just right ... you guessed it – their concentration faces are often expressionless.

So, there's a dog looking at them thinking, 'OK, gimme a clue here. How am I doing?' What's staring back at them is a blank face – and a massive missed opportunity. If you're like this, the chances are you'll rarely be aware it's happening. Try asking someone to remind you.

In combination with facial expressions, our posture tells a tale. When we smile, we melt into a relaxed demeanour. When we scowl, the tension in our facial muscles extends to the rest of the body. We hunch our shoulders, puff out our chests and tighten everything ready for the fight. As a rule of thumb, if you get your face right, the rest of your body will match.

Try this little exercise: smile a huge, beaming smile, but tense the rest of your body in an angry, 'I'm coming to get you' pose. It feels weird, wrong. There's a monumental mismatch that is completely unnatural to us.

Here's the takeaway from years of study: if you want to help your dog understand you, make your facial expressions nice and clear. The rest will follow.

Chapter 6

Get your timing right

Timing is everything, or so the saying goes. I'm not sure it's quite everything in dog training (or this would be a very short book), but it is important. Get your timing wrong and you run the risk of wrecking any progress you're making.

Timing is tricky because getting it right for a dog often feels counter-intuitive to us. The way they connect cause (their behaviour) and effect (our reaction) is so different to the way we see it, meaning people often get it wrong.

Luckily, getting it right is easy when you know how. You might even say it's child's play.

Imagine we're at the side of a busy main road at the edge of a city centre. It's mid-morning. The rush hour has passed but the road is still busy. Because of a traffic-light junction 300 metres away, it's frequently quiet for a minute or two before the lights go green and a new wave of traffic heads towards us.

A young mum is pushing a buggy with her right hand and doing her best to hold onto her three-year-old son, Jack, with her left. She's looking for a spot to cross so she can get to the park opposite and take a breather while Jack eats an ice cream (and joyfully distributes it around his face, hands and clothes). It's worth the hassle of the walk (and the wash) to see how happy it makes him.

Just as Mum decides there isn't time to cross before the next stream of traffic hits, Jack – thinking of only one thing – makes a break for it. He knows where the ice-cream van is and he knows how to get to it. He rips away from his mum's hand and sprints through a gap in the parked cars into the path of an accelerating bus, the weight of 15 small cars.

Mum, horrified, screams and throws herself at him, scrabbling for the back of his T-shirt to drag him back to her as the bus, tyres screeching on the asphalt, skids past. Slewing sideways, it stops with a judder, throwing passengers and bags thudding to the floor. The back wheel, taller than the boy, comes to a stop a toddler's arm-length from him.

Silence. A heavy, ominous, stocktaking silence. Then relief. This time – more by luck than judgement – no one is hurt. The boy is safe.

Two minutes later, his mother's tears begin to subside as she finally releases Jack from her tight embrace. She's been through the full gamut of emotions, and right now she's landed on anger.

'You stupid, stupid boy!' she screams at him. She'll regret it, but can't help it. 'You could have been killed!'

'Sorry, Mummy, sorry, sorry.' It's all Jack can say, spluttering through his tears.

'How many times have I told you? Always stop at the kerb!' She picks him up again and hugs him like she'll never let go.

The moral of this tale is not that we should always stop at kerbs when buses are descending upon us (I'm assuming you know this), but that Jack understands why he is being told off, even though he made his mistake sometime earlier. The behaviour was separated from the consequence but, even so, a three-year-old is still able to connect the two.

That's because Jack's not a dog. Dogs struggle to connect consequences – good or bad – with anything that happens after the event, even by a few seconds, let alone minutes. In order for a dog to understand, the response has to happen while the behaviour is ongoing or, at the very least, immediately afterwards. The term for this phenomenon is *temporal contiguity*. In other words, together in time.

So, let's apply dog logic to the story of Jack and the bus. If the boy were a dog, he'd be looking at his upset and angry mum at the side of the road, long after the bus had departed, and he'd be thinking, 'What on earth is wrong with you?' (Remember, dogs don't understand words.) 'I'm sitting at the side of the kerb, and you're angry. That's confusing,' he'd say. 'When I stepped into the road, you told me off. Now I'm sitting here, doing what you want, but you're also telling me off.'

Put like that, he has a point. Dogs, as you'll see in this book, are very logical when it comes to timing. I've worked with thousands and the truth is I can't remember them all. Some are more memorable than others. One such dog was a little fellow with a big character called Fritz, who lived in Thrapston in Northamptonshire.

My client, Sarah, was living the self-made, single-life dream in a small, detached house on a well-groomed new estate on the edge of town. It was all manicured lawns, BMWs, Audis and cockerpoos. All except for hot-hatch driving, Dachshund-owning, purple-haired Sarah.

'It's lovely here,' she'd said, when I spoke to her on the

phone before our consultation, 'but I've never really fitted in with the Mumsnet set and the rest of them with their WhatsApp groups for local gossip. I've always kept myself to myself, but I need your help with Fritz's barking because I've just had a complaint letter from the council saying I've been reported for a noise nuisance. If it doesn't stop they'll take court action. It doesn't say who reported me, but I'm worried.'

I'd dealt with a council noise complaint before – and many more since – so I knew how upsetting it is for a dog owner to receive one. Even though these letters are a warning, they invariably let the dog owner know the maximum fine is unlimited.

I explained to Sarah that councils have a duty to investigate every complaint and that I'd found the people behind the letters to be very reasonable. Perfection – a silent dog – isn't expected, but excessive barking, and barking at antisocial hours, are where they look to see improvement.

'In fairness, he does bark a lot more than a normal dog,' Sarah said. 'I know dachshunds are famously shouty and he's nervous of anyone who comes into the house. Recently, though, it's got much worse. He's watching out of the bay window now and barking at anyone who passes by until he thinks he's seen them off.'

When the day arrived to visit, I sat down in the front room on an opposite sofa to Sarah and Fritz. I didn't engage with him. I tried my best to start the consultation by shouting over the racket he was making. He really didn't want me to be there and he was making it clear. 'Out! Out! Out!' he barked.

I hoped he'd run out of puff in a few minutes as I was

rather stuck. If I tried to appease him, he'd either get upset as I got closer or, if it had the opposite effect, I'd be rewarding his barking and making things worse in the longer term.

If I told him off, it would only serve to confirm to Fritz that I really was a horrible, scary man. I could have asked Sarah to take him out of the room, but then I'd only have to start all over again. It was a *Catch-22* situation.

The only option was business as usual and wait for him to fizzle out, whereupon I could coach Sarah through praising his quiet behaviour in the right way. It wasn't much, but it was a start. Or at least, it would have been if he'd only shut up for a moment.

Ten minutes on and there was no sign at all that he would ever stop.

'How long does he keep it up for?' I shouted across the coffee table.

'Hours,' was the reply I didn't want to hear. I clearly needed a plan B. And fast.

'Will he listen if you tell him off, Sarah?' I shouted.

'Only for a couple of minutes,' she shouted back. 'But then he's straight back to it.'

'Oh, so he does stop for you, then?' This was music to my beleaguered ears.

'Yes, but as I say, a minute or two, tops.'

A minute or two was loads of time. I'd have settled for ten seconds at this stage. So plan B was clear: ask Sarah to make him stop and then praise him for being a good boy. Timing was key. I'd have to coach her through the praise so she didn't over-excite him. I explained I wanted her to show me how she got him to stop and I'd explain what came next.

Sarah turned to Fritz, put on a schoolmistress face and delivered an equally stern message: 'Fritz . . . NO!'

And that was it. Silence. Schtum. Not a sausage. (There's a sausage-dog pun to be had here, but I'm not going to stoop so low.) For the first time since I'd been in the house, he had stopped barking. I wished I'd hit on plan B ten minutes earlier, but, hey ho, this was good. All we needed to do now was to let him know it was good.

'BAD BOY!'

Oh, hang on. That wasn't in the plan. Before I could stop her, Sarah unleashed all her frustration on the poor little dog.

'This nice man,' she shouted, without taking her eyes off him and wagging a finger behind herself in my direction, 'has come here just to help you, and all you can do is sit there and bark your bloody head off! You bad, BAD BOY!'

Then she slumped back in the sofa, seemingly contented, turned to me and said, 'OK. Now what?'

I didn't know whether to laugh or cry. Poor Fritz would be sitting there, thinking: 'What just happened here? I tried to get rid of the nasty man and you said nothing—' (I always imagine how dogs would talk and – forgive me if you're from that great country – in my head there's no way this dachshund called Fritz isn't speaking with a German accent) '—Then you shouted at me for barking. So, I was quiet . . . Next, you shouted at me for being quiet. You are crazy, woman!'

And with that, the little dog – more scared than before – fired up once again.

'Out! Out! Out!'

'See?' Sarah shouted, throwing her hands in the air. 'He's crazy!'

So far I hadn't taught Sarah or Fritz very much, but I had at least learned a valuable lesson myself. Always tell the client what to do in advance because, when everything happens so quickly like this, there's no time to interject.

The lesson I'd meant to teach was about timing and Sarah had ably demonstrated the perils of getting it wrong. It's easy to do because, as humans, we hang on to our emotions for such a long time. We keep on talking about a bad thing that happened long after the moment has gone.

Dogs, on the other hand, move on immediately. Or at least they would if we'd let them. It's all part of how dogs live in the moment. It sounds a lot like mindfulness to me, and no one ever needed to send a dog on a mindfulness course. They know too much.

You may have heard people saying that you must never tell dogs off after the event. It's true, but it doesn't mean you should stand around doing nothing either, particularly if the bad behaviour has now stopped. As soon as it is over, provided they choose something better to do instead, you can flip into reward mode. You don't have to – and you shouldn't – wait. A reward can be praise or affection (my go-to in most cases), food (good if your dog is so minded), toys or anything else pleasant that works for your dog.

Occasionally, I've heard an owner say they ignored their badly behaved dog for hours after some incident. What happens then, invariably, is that the dog will start acting out of character, moping about and looking glum. It's typically taken by owners as a sign that he knows he's done wrong. That's not what's happening at all. Rather, he's reading the situation, the faces and the body language, and he's certainly thinking something's wrong. *Mum's not happy, maybe with me, but who knows?* Whatever he's thinking, he's no closer to understanding what's actually going on. He certainly wouldn't be wondering if it had anything to do with his grabbing the parish newsletter delivery lady's fingers and trying to drag her through the letterbox and into the hallway. (Everyone running around screaming hadn't helped.) Of course not. That kerfuffle happened hours ago, after all, and Mum is upset now.

It's an extreme example, although I've heard worse, but you get the point. People hang on to emotions longer than dogs hang on to delivery people. That isn't to say dogs don't remember things. On the contrary, they have great memories.

The problem is, we can't use language to explain what they did wrong. With people, we do it all the time. 'Sit down, we need to talk about yesterday . . .' It sounds ominous already. We can talk about the past, explain our feelings, suggest how the other person might behave in a better way to make everyone's lives easier, and the list goes on. But, of course, this doesn't work with dogs. We're running different operating systems (languages) and different hardware (brains). There's no way we can access their memory directly, nor they ours.

So, it's not that dogs can't remember things – I'd be out of a job if they couldn't – and nor are they stupid. It's just that they're wired differently. To communicate with them, we have to keep it simple, match our response to the exact moment something is happening and stay mentally agile so that we switch with the behaviour. Do that and I'd say you'll have mastered something that most dog people don't get right in a lifetime's ownership: the art of timing.

Chapter 7

Mark and reward – fixed-reward schedule

No discussion about timing and dog training would be complete without reference to clickers. A clicker is a small, hand-held device that uses a spring steel leaf in a plastic box to make a distinctive 'click-click' sound.

They've been in common use by dog trainers since the 1980s, following the publication of *Don't Shoot the Dog!* by Karen Pryor. This book is essential reading for any would-be dog trainer. I rarely use a clicker myself, although I do use the principle behind them almost every time I'm training a dog. There are pros and cons to clickers, but before we discuss them let's examine the right way to use them. To do that, it's really useful to look at the backstory. Are you sitting comfortably? Then I shall begin.

Once upon a time in a magical land called Harvard, there lived a psychologist called B.F. Skinner who, in the 1930s and 1940s, used the phrase 'operant conditioning' to describe how animals learn, by trial and error, to behave in a way that earns a reward. Professor Skinner is famous for putting lab rats in a box and letting them discover how to get food treats for themselves. The rats were the operants – operating a small lever that caused food to be dropped into the box. As a result, the rats became conditioned (trained) through choosing to behave in a certain way time and again.

Away from the mystical world of Skinner's laboratory and a couple of decades later, during the 1960s, dolphin trainers – aware of operant conditioning – had a specific problem to overcome: how to train a dolphin to do tricks in the middle of a swimming pool when the fish that was used to reward them was in a bucket at the side: if you take the bucket into the pool, you'll be mobbed; if you sit at the side of the pool with the goodies, why would any self-respecting dolphin leave you to go and do tricks over there? How would you get them to understand that 'over there' is where you want them to perform, but 'back here' is where the reward will happen?

What was needed was a device to mark the precise moment the dolphin earned a fish and to bridge the time gap until the trainer was able to give it to them. The answer to the conundrum came in the form of a marker signal (or 'bridging stimulus', in psychology-speak). A marker is a very quick, clear signal that says, 'Bingo! That's what I want and I promise to reward you for it as soon as I can.' In the case of the dolphin trainers, a whistle fit the bill perfectly.

Here's how we might use one to train a dolphin. First, we need to make the connection for the dolphin that the 'peep' of the whistle means fish is coming. To do this, we might sit at the side of the pool throwing our dolphin bits of fish and blowing one clear 'peep' as the fish is thrown.

Let's say we throw a dozen or so pieces in a session and we ran a few sessions over a period of a week. Pretty soon, our smart dolphin's thinking, 'If I hear that whistle, I'm on a winner.' Whistle = fish. At this stage we haven't even begun to reward behaviour, but what we have done is create our marker signal.

The next stage involves us doing nothing for quite a while. Our clever dolphin – let's call her Dolly – is going to hang around with us at the side of the pool. Why wouldn't she? Eventually, though, she'll realise that the whistle isn't going to sound and no fish will appear. At that point she goes swimming off around the pool, probably in the dolphin equivalent of a huff.

Let's say that we now want Dolly to figure out that if she jumps out of the water, we'll reward her. Waiting for her to jump fully clear of the water could lead to a very long wait. Instead, let's say we reward her for putting her nose out of the water and then encourage her to give us more and more of that, progressively, until she's jumping. Here's how we do it. We sit back and wait until she nudges her nose out of the water by a few inches, quite randomly. We blow the whistle: 'PEEP!' As quick as a flash, Dolly the dolphin makes the connection (fish inbound) and swims back to us to get it.

Nice though it would be to think that Dolly would know straight away what she did right, the truth is that she probably won't have done so yet and she'll swim around trying different things that don't work. Eventually, though, she happens to poke her nose out of the water again and – 'PEEP!' – the game is on. The more she pokes her nose out, the more the whistle blows. As far as Dolly is concerned, she's turning us into a fish-dispensing machine and all she has to do is stick her nose out of the water by a few inches.

It's not jumping, but it's a start. Just as Dolly has figured out the trick, we withhold the whistle (and the fish) when she nudges out of the water. We're taking the first steps to shape her behaviour. Dolly tries a little harder to earn the fish by pushing her whole head out of the water and 'PEEP!' – joy of joys – the game recommences. From now on, nothing less than this far out of the water will do the trick. If she tries hard, she's rewarded. It's nice and clear.

Although the jump and the fish are separated by a few seconds, we've bridged the gap with our marker signal (the blow of the whistle) and then we've gone one better, shaping the behaviour into something bigger and better than we started with. Over days and weeks, Dolly begins enthusiastically jumping all the way out of the water to prompt the whistle and earn her fish.

The dog training applications are obvious and yet it took a couple of decades more before operant conditioning truly caught on by using a clicker instead of a whistle; presumably because dog trainers were already using whistles for other things.

The principles are the same as with Dolly the dolphin. First, we get the dog used to the sound of the click, making the association with a treat coming immediately after – and after a few sessions of doing little more than that, we withhold clicks (and treats) until our dog does something desirable.

If necessary, we can lure our dog into position to speed things up (we'll talk in more depth about luring, later). We're always working to the same principle: good behaviour = click = treat. We then shape the behaviour by withholding the clicks until we're offered a better version of the behaviour. In dog training terms, that might, for example, be a faster sit, a more solid down, a longer stay, or even a harder bite from a police dog. The possibilities are endless.

There are many advantages to the clicker method. It's a clever yet simple way to bridge the gap between behaviour and reward if, indeed, there's a gap to bridge. (Dogs tend not to be trained out of reach in a swimming pool, of course, but there are times when we may want to train them at a distance – recall springs to mind).

The sound of a clicker is consistent. It marks the moment of good behaviour in a clinical, non-emotional way. It's also precise in its ability, if used correctly, to signal split-second moments of good behaviour. This, in turn, makes things crystal-clear for the dog. 'Oh, that's what you want. You like THIS.'

For all that, I hardly ever use a clicker because there are disadvantages. For a start they are a bit fiddly and in practice giving someone a device to press at the same time as holding a dog lead and dosing out treats is rather like patting your head and rubbing your tummy in circles at the same time. So for example, if you're in front of your dog teaching him something quick and easy, such as 'sit', it makes more sense to reward good behaviour directly. Instead of saying, 'That's good, but hang on and I'll give you a treat in a sec' (e.g. with a marker), why wouldn't you simply say, 'That's good, here's a treat' (or praise, a favourite toy and so on). It's clearer, more direct and much more likely to get quicker results.

Also, the consistent sound of a click, which takes the emotion out of our response, is a double-edged sword. If your voice is likely to be gruff or unhappy-sounding when you're marking good behaviour, then yes, sure, a click is better. But if you can manage to sound happy when you're offering praise – and I'd estimate that more than 90 per cent of us have no problem with that – then why wouldn't we want emotion in the marker signal?

There's also a side issue with clickers that hardly matters in the real world, but is something I've seen in the dog training class environment. You can imagine the scene when, say, ten clicker-trained dogs are all hearing an owner click away at a dog further down the hall and confusion reigns, because most clickers sound the same. It's why I'm not a fan of clickers in classes.

So, we have a situation where a marker signal can be really useful, but a clicker isn't always ideal. What's the answer? A marker word. For many years, I've used my voice to create a marker by employing one word which I keep special and only use to mark good moments. The technique was taught to me by a Scottish trainer and it's pretty simple. 'Good!' was the word he taught me and I've stuck with it ever since. Curiously, because accents rub off on me quite readily, a Scottish-sounding 'GUID!' is the way it always comes out. I say it in an excited, happy pitch and the combination of the unique-sounding word and the pitch sets it apart from run-of-the-mill speech.

Provided I'm disciplined in only using that special sound as a marker, it has all the advantages of a clicker and none of the disadvantages. It's hands-free, it carries happy emotion and it is always available exactly when I need it (unless I lose my voice, but that happens way less frequently than I'd lose a clicker). The timing is precise because there aren't the complex motor skills involved in clicking and juggling a lead and treats at the same time and I can even use it in an environment with other dogs because my voice – and my choice of marker word – is unique. It's clicker training without the clicker. What's not to love?

Chapter 8
Intermittent-reward schedules

We need to talk about fixed versus intermittent-reward schedules. I realise it probably sounds about as dry as four-day-old sourdough toast, but bear with me because if you can crack this concept – and it's not hard, I promise – you'll be well on your way not only to a dog that is well behaved, but one that's addicted to good behaviour.

We're going to get to grips with this concept through the magic of toast. Yup, toast.

But before that, let's consider how new behaviours develop. If we're teaching a puppy to sit on command, we might choose to reward her by giving a little treat every time she does it. Sit-treat, sit-treat, sit-treat and so on. She's beginning to get the idea. If she sits, we reward her. Remember, a reward can be anything that feels good; it doesn't have to be an edible treat. Pretty quickly, a habit is forming. Through days and weeks of repetition, she's made a very clear connection between sitting and getting rewarded for it.

Now, she's offering a sit whether or not you ask her. When

you do ask, she's doing it so quickly it seems automatic. We're on a fixed-reward schedule, sometimes expressed as a fixed ratio: one treat for each sit, hence 1:1.

We're halfway there. The fixed-reward schedule was phase one of our reward-based training. You've done a great job of creating a solid new habit over hundreds of repetitions, but if you stop giving the rewards now, there's a good chance the behaviour will simply fade away. It becomes 'extinguished'. We discussed behaviour extinction when we talked about ignoring bad behaviour. Sadly, it happens all too often in this scenario too, because, unless we're forewarned, it's tempting to think it's a case of job done and we stop the treats, whereupon everything starts to unravel.

If you're using rewards to train new behaviours (and you should), you need to know how to fade them out too, because no one wants to spend the rest of their life walking with a big bag of treats in one hand and a lead attached to a fat dog in the other. We need a way to lock the new behaviour in place so that it's robust and not likely to fade away if you don't reward it every single time.

That's where a variable-reward schedule comes in. It's the psychology of addiction, both in dogs and humans. That makes it sound bad, but it doesn't have to be and a dog addicted to good behaviour sounds pretty good to me.

I'm not sure I'd say it's an addiction as such, but I love toast. There's a deli near me that sells a brown sourdough bloomer called the Cotswold Crunch. I daren't tell my mum how much it costs because: 1) Although I've been living abroad (that is, outside Yorkshire) for longer than I care to admit, I still like to think I'm careful with money and ...

2) My mum's getting on a bit and she's not entirely au fait with the value of things these days. Why would she be? The last time she bought a house was in 1962 and she probably thinks you can get a whole row of West Yorkshire terraced two-up-two-downs for the price of a Cotswold Crunch.

It's lovely bread, but here's the thing – it's not always available when I pop into the deli. The baker delivers at about 9am and, when the last one has gone, it's gone. I do quite like the pot-luck effect, though: if there's one left, it makes my day (I'm easily pleased). The uncertainty is a little addictive. If the bakers are restricting supply to 'treat me mean and keep me keen', they're evil geniuses, because it works.

Team a thick slice of Cotswold Crunch toast with some smashed avocado and extra virgin olive oil and there's a perfect lunch. I buy an avocado occasionally and forget it's in the fridge. It's not quite ripe when I get it and so I stow it away and lose track. Imagine my delight when I walk in with my prized bread and check the fridge to discover the secret avocado stash from last Saturday's Waitrose trip. Jackpot!

Note that it's the uncertainty, the pleasant surprise effect that makes it doubly rewarding. If I had Cotswold Crunch and avocado every day for breakfast, lunch and dinner I'd be sick of the sight of it by now. But because of the jackpot effect, I'm ever so slightly addicted. I love it when I have it, but I can't have it every time and I start to crave it.

That's the point of a variable reward schedule. I do the same things many times – visit the deli, check out the fridge – and sometimes I am rewarded, but often I'm not.

Slot machines and lotteries are other great examples of variable-reward schedules in action. They become addictive because – even though we know the odds are stacked heavily against us – we crave the jackpot effect.

Incidentally, the wait is part of the game. With a slot machine, the time it takes the wheels to roll around is long enough for the brain to register the anticipation of pleasure. It's all based on the knowledge that the random rewards of gambling are much more seductive than a more predictable fixed-reward schedule.

To prove the point, let's consider a hypothetical slot machine that works on a fixed-reward schedule. Each time a pound is pushed through the slot and the lever pulled, a pound and a penny are churned back out. Whoopee-doo. We're playing the only slot machine in the world guaranteed to make us (not the owners) money. It should be exciting, but in fact it would prove pretty boring. There's a reason real slots are variable schedule (they drop random jackpots), and the drinks are free. A fixed-schedule machine, like our hypothetical one, which paid you to be there while you paid for your own drinks, would be very dreary indeed. If there's one thing Vegas isn't, it's dreary. But they do know a thing or two about extracting money (repeatedly) from people by making them feel good.

Social media acts in the same way. It works on a variable-reward schedule and the reward it offers is perhaps the most intoxicating to humans: approval.

Note, too, that the whole point of variable schedules is that the reward happens randomly. The ratio moves not from 1:1 to a rigid 1:3 or 1:5, but to a variable, never-know-when-it's-coming ratio of behaviour to reward. And it has to happen frequently enough that the subject (the dog, in our case) believes that it's going to happen sooner or later and so it's still worth trying for.

Let's now have a look at how to incorporate variable schedules within dog training. We can start by introducing variation into the delay between our dog giving us the behaviour we want and the moment the reward arrives. We can do this by beginning to hold off with the treat.

Bobby the Border collie puppy is smart, like most of his kind. He's also eager to learn. This turns out to be a double-edged sword because, while he's quick to learn the good stuff, he's equally quick at picking up bad stuff, too.

Recently he's learned what 'sit' means. He picked this up on a fixed schedule and a treat has been almost fired into his mouth by his super-keen owner the instant the first wisp of fur on his bottom touches the carpet. The problem we've got now is that Bobby has decided 'sit' means dip your bottom to the floor, then pop straight back up again because the quicker you do, the quicker there's another sit/treat cycle coming. Bobby's crafty, huh?

The problem is that Bobby's owners were too keen to please. Once he'd got the hang of sitting for a treat, they could have introduced the tiniest delay between the sit and the reward. A second would have been plenty to start with. The message here is: sit and stay sitting for a second and you'll get this treat (but you cannot have it if you get up).

I would randomise it – sometimes an immediate reward, sometimes a slight delay. Either way, sitting (and staying put) gets it for him. Once he'd got the hang of that, I'd extend the delay but still on a variable basis: no delay . . . two seconds . . . one second . . . no delay . . . three seconds . . . one second and so on. If you're looking for a pattern, there isn't one, other than I'm stretching the delay over time and lots of repeats.

Tomorrow I might throw in a couple of four-second delays and so on. It creates a super-steady dog which, like a gambler at a slot machine, is going to stay put until the next time the jackpot drops. There's a big difference, though: your dog will look way happier. Interacting with you is much more fun than being addicted to slots.

The next stage is a variable-reward schedule proper because we're going to start throwing in the odd 'sit' command that is not rewarded. Mostly, the dog gets a treat still, but it's not guaranteed. Again, it's unpredictable – random – but always worth trying for.

This is a leap of faith for owners. Not rewarding good behaviour feels wrong after lots of training, and if you're British – bad luck – our famous sense of fair play makes it doubly vexing to withhold credit where it's due. But trust me, the first time you withhold a treat, your dog training will not come crashing down around you. It's quite the opposite: typically, dogs try a little harder when the expected treat doesn't turn up. Try it for yourself.

So, you've moved from a fixed schedule through variable time intervals to variable rewards themselves. That's the right order to progress.

A quick clarification. You may reasonably ask why, if variable-reward schedules are so powerful, we wouldn't simply start that way and skip fixed schedules altogether? It's because we need to show our dog which behaviour we want first, and to reassure him that he's on the right track.

The best way to do that is to reward the right thing every

time initially. Let's go back to our genius puppy, Bobby, when he first learned what his owners wanted from him. On a variable schedule, he's only going to get a random reward for sitting. Bobby sits but gets nothing again and again. Finally, he sits and gets a treat, then nothing again, nothing and so on.

He's trying to figure out by trial and error what on earth the human word 'sit' means. Clearly, he surmises, it cannot be the putting-your-bottom-on-the-floor thing, because he hardly ever gets a treat for that. Start him on a variable schedule, and he'll be bobbing up and down forever, trying to second-guess what's required. Alternatively, start him with a treat every time on a fixed schedule so that he makes the connection quickly, then move to a variable schedule to lock in his good behaviour, and you're onto a winner. Plus, imagine the saving you'll make on treats. (Did I mention I'm an ex-pat Yorkshireman?)

At this point I think it's worth clarifying a few bits of terminology. We've already discussed rewarding good behaviour (and people accidentally rewarding unwanted behaviours, too). To reward a dog, I'll do anything that's safe if I judge it will feel good for the dog. If he likes the feeling, he'll give me more of the desired behaviour. That includes food rewards, but also toys and expressions of affection (as signalled by tone of voice, touch and body language). Rewards and treats aren't synonymous. Treats, for most dogs, are rewarding but not all rewards are treats. It pays to keep an open mind.

I went to see a family once with a mixed-breed brindle-coloured American bulldog/mastiff called Bruce. He pulled on the lead and had a few other little issues, which were all bread and butter for me. Early on in the consultation the family told me he wasn't one for treats and, outside in particular, he would spit food out if they tried to give him any.

We cracked on with some training and went back to the house for a cup of tea. We'd been playing with him, using his favourite tug toy as a reward when he was good. I thought we'd progressed well, so was surprised when the mother of the family asked, 'Do you think he's trainable?' It seemed a silly question because he'd very obviously been responding well to training. But these weren't silly people, by any means.

'Yes, absolutely. He's doing fine,' I confirmed. 'Why do you ask?'

'We were told by a local dog trainer that he was untrainable,' the mum said.

I was a little taken aback. It was the first time I'd heard a dog branded untrainable before, though I've heard it a few times since. I cannot fix everything all the time, despite my very best efforts, but that's not to say that someone, somewhere can't find a way I didn't think of. We're all fallible.

'Untrainable? How come?' I asked.

'She told us that we had to use rewards, meaning food, but he didn't respond to the treats she had with her. She came here three times in the end, each time with better food. On the last occasion, she had some liver that she'd been marinating in some barbecue sauce concoction overnight. "This will do the trick!" she said. Apparently, it had never failed, but Bruce took one look at it, sniffed and turned his nose up. I knew he would. She said he was "untrainable" and walked out.'

'Well, if you insist on treats as the reward, he may be, yes,'

I replied, trying my best to hide my surprise and look professional. 'But that's kind of missing the point. There's no sense rewarding him with something he doesn't want, but if he'd do anything for a tug on his toy with you, well, there you go. Use that.'

The truth is, we're all motivated by different things. Dogs too. Offering to ply me with spinach if I come to your house and do a good job is, frankly, not going to fill me with warm, fuzzy feelings. Thanks for the offer and all that. Custard creams might be a better ploy but, in truth – and as corny as this might sound – a heartfelt thanks at the end of a consultation and the feeling of satisfaction as I drive off into the sunset knowing I was able to help someone and their dog is actually more rewarding than biscuits. (But don't let that discourage you from offering baked goods, too, should we meet some happy day.) Save the goodies until I've done a bit of work, though, because waving a packet of biscuits at me on the doorstep when I arrive and saying, 'Look what we've got if you're a good boy,' feels a bit like bribery.

So it is with dog training. The reward should appear either during the good behaviour or at the tail end of it, but not before (unless you're luring a dog into position – more on that in a moment).

* * *

Do you know anyone who has to rattle a treats tin every night to get their dog back in from the garden after the last time they've been out? They may be kidding themselves that they're rewarding good behaviour, but they're not. They're bribing. The difference? Take away the treats tin and what have you got? Nothing, presumably. We're aiming for a dog that thinks, 'I'll do the work first, you can pay me later,' and not, 'If you don't bribe me, I'm not listening.'

Tempting though it is to say that bribery isn't dog training, I have to say that's not quite correct. The truth is much worse: when you bribe a dog, you're training them all right, but to be disobedient.

Where does this leave luring a dog into position with a treat? I'm very clear on the distinction. Let's take the example of teaching a dog to lie down by holding a treat securely in our hand and letting her sniff, then moving it down to the ground. The dog's nose follows the hand down, her bottom is initially wagging in the air, but as she decides to rest her back legs and lie down properly, we open our hand and she gets rewarded with the treat.

Note that she only gets the treat once she's lying down. We gave her a clue as to what we wanted and then marked the precise moment she lay down with a treat. As we repeat the exercise, she'll start to lie down more and more quickly.

At this stage, we're on a fixed-reward schedule – rewarding every correct 'down' – and when we're sure she's got it, we'll move to a variable schedule, rewarding it randomly. Very soon, she'll be lying down when we ask, whether there's a treat there or not. We'll have moved from luring her into position to only sporadically giving her a treat for a job well done.

That's the difference between luring and bribing. Luring is a means to an end, a temporary stage we pass through to get a solid behaviour that stands on its own without the need of a treat every time. It's the opposite of training for disobedience.

In the previous example – when we were teaching a dog

to lie down by luring her – there was something missing, something that almost all first-time dog trainers would be doing at this stage. I wonder if you noticed what it was? At no point did I mention a word command, such as 'down' or 'lie'. I didn't leave it out for clarity. Rather, it's just that I don't use commands at this stage. There's a time for introducing them and it's toward the end of the process.

The reason for this is that I'm aiming to bed in the new behaviour and get our dog to understand what I'd like her to do before I start throwing human words around. Remember that words don't come as naturally to dogs as they do to us and, while she's engaging her brain to figure out how the game works, it's not at all helpful if we're bombarding her with audible distractions at the same time. It's all too much.

I prefer to think of commands as labels. When she's understood the game (we point towards the floor, she lies down properly, she's gets a treat), then – and only then – do we tell her the name of the game. In other words, this is when we start saying 'down' – as we point. She had started to recognise the hand gesture from the luring we did initially and now we're pairing something new to it – the sound of the word 'down'.

From now on, the soundtrack to the training is 'down', delivered in a happy voice. Because she already knows the game, she hears the command (the 'stimulus', in psychology-speak) and thinks, 'Oh, that!' and throws herself at the floor. To use the correct terminology, we've put the behaviour under stimulus control. In other words, we've created a word-label that we can use to trigger the new behaviour whenever we want – on cue, so to speak.

Explained like this, hopefully it makes sense. The problem is that it's counter-intuitive for humans. We talk. It's what we do a lot. There seems to be an unwritten law of the universe that states that any person in possession of a puppy and a treat shall start shouting 'sit', 'down', 'siddown' and many other words until the poor animal is completely befuddled.

Do your dog a favour: make the effort to keep your commands for the last phase of training (it's harder than you think), and reserve your voice for praise until then.

A dog whistle is the same as a voice command, to all intents and purposes. It's a unique sound associated with an action. Whistles are much favoured by gundog trainers and hill farmers for good reasons; the shrill sound of a proper dog whistle carries well outdoors and in windy conditions, almost certainly carrying further than the human voice. There's an argument that it scares game and livestock less than the human voice too, and takes emotion out of the sound, and is, therefore, more consistent.

Like a clicker, there's nothing magical about a whistle. It's a tool of the trade and, as such, how you use it is important. If you've got a recall problem, for example, I think there's little merit in buying a whistle as a quick fix. That said, I've lost count of the number of times someone has told me their dog responded well to a whistle in the first week or so, but then never again. I put that down to curiosity: 'Why is Mum making that funny sound?' Once they get used to it, if everything else has remained the same, they soon sadly revert to ignoring their owners.

Personally, I'm inclined not to use a whistle most of the time because, although they do undoubtedly have advantages in some applications, for most pet-dog training I find I can get the results I need without one, so there's little benefit. The downside to using a whistle is that it's one more thing to take on a walk and potentially lose. With a decent lanyard, you're unlikely to drop a whistle but I'm a great believer in the adage that if it can happen, sooner or later it will, and if a lost whistle means no recall, you're in trouble.

My advice is that if you're going to use a whistle, always train a recall voice command in parallel with the whistle, so you can use either. I'd start with a consistent voice command and, after a few weeks, add a whistle signal immediately before or after each call so that your dog associates the two things: peep-peep = 'Come!' As with voices, it's important to keep the whistle blows consistent (the number of blows per command and the length of the blow, for example). Soon enough, you'll find your whistle works as a standalone command. Arguably, that's the best of two worlds.

One last thought on voice commands. The word you choose is up to you. Because we're programming your dog to match a behaviour with a word, it follows that the word can be anything. Choose wisely, though, and then stick to your choices consistently. Words that sound similar aren't going to help your dog to understand, so think about the sound of them before you start training. 'Sit down', 'lie down' and 'get down' at least begin in different ways, but they could easily be changed to 'sit', 'down' and 'off', for example, making things so much clearer. Dogs like things to be clear.

Chapter 9
Generalisation

Lightbulb moments happen quite a lot in my one-to-one consultations with dog owners. Often, I can predict when they are going to happen because there are aspects of how dogs think that are real eye-openers if you don't already know about them. I love sharing these little gems because I remember the delight I felt when I first heard about them.

Some lightbulb moments surprise me, though. I was in the kitchen of a country house in the Chilterns many years ago, doing a puppy consultation, when one such surprise happened. I don't do so many puppy consultations these days, which is a shame. Since the advent of *Dogs Behaving (Very) Badly* on TV, I'm seen more often as the guy who sorts out dogs' behavioural problems. To a large extent I always was, but I used to run more puppy one-to-ones, too, where the emphasis was on creating the very best start in life for dogs. In effect, I was the 'preventing problems' guy, rather than Mr Fix It.

So, there I was, holding court around a kitchen table, explaining about something known to dog trainers as 'generalisation', when the whole family erupted in exclamations of, 'No wonder!' and, 'That's why!'

It turned out that 12-year-old Tom had been busy in his bedroom for weeks, training Flossie the puppy to within an inch of her life. Flossie was Tom's first dog and he'd taken his responsibility very seriously indeed. I was there because it had been agreed Tom could have a puppy if he trained it properly. Unfortunately, a much-vaunted dog obedience show in the sitting room that Tom had planned a couple of days before my arrival hadn't exactly gone to plan.

Tom had been perfecting his 'sit', 'down', 'stay' and 'give-me-a-paw' routines with Border collie, Flossie. She was a clever girl and, in Tom's room, they'd been training hard for three whole weeks, which, as everyone knows, is a very long time indeed when you're 12. It's longer still when you're 13 dog-weeks old. Tom had thrown himself at the task with electric enthusiasm. Dog training had become his new special interest and he'd been obsessing about every book and website he could get his hands on, long before getting Flossie. There was no way she was going to be anything other than perfect, he told himself, with the kind of self-belief that exists only in kids.

With the whole family amassed on sofas in front of him, Tom proudly introduced Flossie the wonder-puppy. It was show time.

Flossie wandered around the room, seemingly paying no attention to Tom. She'd only been in the sitting room – normally reserved for vicars and insufferable relatives – three times in her short life and no one had her taught her (or the insufferable relatives), how to behave here. Tom proclaimed his first command. 'Flossie,' he shouted, with the panache of a circus ringmaster, 'Sit!' Flossie did nothing. 'Flossie, sit!' he repeated, less confidently. Still nothing. 'Flosseee . . . ? He was desperate now and it was clear she was paying no attention at all. One last try. Tom dug deep, put on his best dog-trainer voice and gave it one last shot. 'Flossie!' She looked at him for the first time. This was good . . . 'Sit!'

Without any flicker of recognition on her face, but still watching Tom, she started to lower her back tentatively towards the floor. She paused, hovering with her bottom a quarter of an inch above the parquet flooring and, with Tom and the amassed family watching with bated breath, promptly emptied the entire contents of her bladder on the wooden floor, sending Tom's mum scurrying to the kitchen for a jumbo roll of paper towel and special (for which, read expensive) puppy-smell neutralising spray.

No matter. The show must go on and Tom wasn't for quitting. Not quite yet, at least. Parquet decontaminated, he started again. A different tack was required, he reasoned (clever lad). 'Flossie, come!' he called, and Flossie ran back in the room, over the parquet and landed in front of him, on the rug between the Chesterfield sofa and the Victorian bay window that looked out onto the front lawns.

So far, so good. Tom looked down at the little puppy and decided to go for gold. He'd trained the fastest 'down' in the Home Counties, or so he thought, and so he figured this was his best chance to redeem them both. She could do it. She'd done it hundreds of times in his bedroom. It never failed.

'Flossie . . .' he said, with just a hint of trepidation in his voice. Flossie started to sniff the ground and circle in front of him. He shrugged it off. 'Flossie . . .' There was an imaginary drum roll in Tom's head . . . 'Down!'

The little puppy continued to circle for a moment and then came to a stop. She hung her bottom over the floor, tucked her tummy underneath herself, curved her back and . . .

'Oh, dear God, no!' shouted Tom's mum, 'not on the Persian rug—' But it was too late. Flossie produced the biggest number two anyone had ever seen from such a small puppy and extruded it, Mister Whippee-style, in the centre of Tom's impromptu stage. Had the adjudicators for the *Guinness Book of Records* been there to witness it, Flossie would surely have been crowned a world-record holder on the spot. 'Never work with animals or children!' joked Tom's father, somewhat unhelpfully, after the boy as he headed for the boot room, puppy in arms.

Poor Tom. He wasn't the first dog trainer to see his efforts fall apart, and he won't be the last. He'd done almost everything right, too, because, by all accounts, Flossie was perfect in the bedroom when he ran her through the tricks he'd trained. She never put a paw wrong. In the living room, however, it was a whole new ball game.

Where Tom had gone wrong was failing to transfer the good work he'd done in one place to a number of other places before putting it to the test. It's called generalisation. Most people do generalisation effortlessly. If you're an accountant, for example, you can change companies and hit the ground running when you start at the new place because it's easy for us to take skills we've learned and reapply them elsewhere. Easy for us, but not so much for dogs.

With dogs, and puppies in particular, I typically start in one place with a fixed, then variable schedule of rewards and, once it's looking good, I start doing the same training – from the start if necessary – in three or four different locations. We're moving from 'sit means sit in this one place', to 'sit means sit . . . here, here, here and here'.

When, typically after somewhere between five and ten locations, your dog understands that 'sit' means 'sit' anywhere, including new places that she's never seen before, then we can say that the training is generalised. That's the only thing Tom had been missing and it's what caused the lightbulbs to switch on around the room during the consultation. If he'd done training in his bedroom, in the kitchen, the boot room, the garden and – you've guessed it – in the sitting room, he (and Flossie) would have stood a much better chance.

Chapter 10

Excitement is the problem

'Calm down! Laughing turns to crying.' I wonder how many times I heard my mum say that to me when I was a kid, usually when I was playing with my sister. Hundreds or perhaps thousands of times we were told to settle down before it all went wrong.

Mums just seem to know these things. Maybe there's a software package, a kind of Mummy Wisdom v1.0 that comes bundled with the hardware when they have their first-born child. All I know is that, as killjoy as it seemed when I was a kid, she was almost always right. Laughing – or at least over-excitement – usually did tip over into some form of unpleasantness. I'd point out, of course, that it was all Andrea's fault, but Mum was always disappointingly fair.

Fast-forward three decades and I'm studying dog training and behaviour, gleaning knowledge from wherever I can, from books and course materials, and watching proper dog trainers at work. When I throw myself into something, I never do it by halves. 'If a job's worth doing, it's worth doing well,' was my maternal grandfather's motto. He died a few months before I was born, but my childhood was full of his presence. And not just the physical remnants, such as the plant pots bearing his initials that he made and fired during breaks in his job at the brickworks, or the how to grow sweet-pea books in Grandma's outhouse loft.

Those things were certainly everywhere, but it was more than that. At times, it seemed that I was turning into a version of this legendary man I'd never known. 'My dad used to do that,' my mum would say about some new mannerism I'd developed as a teenager. She'd mention it to my grandma and the verdict would invariably be: 'He's just like him.'

I asked my dad about him once. 'He was a good man, was Sid,' he said. 'I remember when your mum brought me home to meet her parents and I thought, "Oh, it's you!" because I recognised him from around town. Everyone had a lot of respect for him and I was a bit overawed really. But he was all right, you know.' (Again, if you're not familiar with Yorkshire folk, it's worth pointing out that 'all right' is pretty much the highest form of praise you'll ever hear. Nothing in Yorkshire is ever 'amazing' or 'fabulous' – perish the thought.)

Looking back, I think the just-like-your-granddad theme was partly wishful thinking, an always-there longing to bring him back, but also there was probably a sense in which it was very real. Genetics are a powerful thing and I guess I was – am – like him. It's a sobering thought that I'm older now than he was when he died. Whether it's nature or nurture that's responsible (something we'll be talking about in the book), I do think that if a job's worth doing, it's worth doing well. If I take on a new special interest, I want to know everything about it. That's what happened with dog behaviour.

When I set about learning everything I could about it,

what everyone seemed to agree on was that for dogs to be obedient, you have to rev them up a bit, make them excited. 'Don't be afraid to use a bright and happy voice,' they'd say. 'Wave your arms around! You've got to be the most interesting thing in the park to get your dog's attention!' It's a mantra that I still hear a lot today. I call it the 'whoopee-doo approach' and you'll find it in most puppy classes. There is a place for excitement in dog training. Take agility, flyball and competition obedience dogs, for example. Slow and dull isn't going to win prizes.

In the world of working dogs, too, lack of excitement isn't just undesirable, it can be downright dangerous. A number of police forces in the UK experimented with Rottweilers a few years ago. I was a Rottweiler owner myself and I was keen to hear how they got on. I had another vested interest – I'd recently been a victim of crime. In a particularly upsetting burglary, the tie pin my grandma had gifted to her husband on their wedding day, and then left to me after she died, was taken from me. It was never recovered. Call me unkind, but the idea that the little darlings responsible might one day be 'apprehended' by a police Rottweiler wasn't exactly unappealing.

I tracked down a police sergeant who was head of the force's dog section. He had many years' experience with German shepherds, but he was now on his first and, as it turned out, his last Rottweiler.

'I bet they're awesome police dogs, aren't they?' I asked, failing to conceal my amateurish bias.

'Not really,' he said. 'When they bite, my God do you know about it, even through a padded training suit. So, that's true. But they are so hard to control. Not physically, although that is a bit of an issue, but no, mentally they are hard work, stubborn. This one' – he gestured to the back of his van – 'his answer to everything is "Make me!" He's on his way out actually. We're not going to keep him. I made my mind up the other day when we turned up to a job and he wouldn't get out of the van.'

I was all ears.

'I got called to a pub fight at a place that's always full of ne'er-do-wells. So, off we go, grade one response, blue lights and, when I get there, I'm the first officer on the scene. Just me and numpty-boy, here. You never know what you're going to find when you get there – nine times out of ten, a pub fight is all handbags at dawn. It's a case of, "Here we go again", so, a bit of presence and a few choice words, and it all fizzles out.

'But this was different. When you've been in the job for as long as I have, you can sense it as soon as you drive up. It had already spilled out into the car park, two big groups going at each other. There were chairs flying, glasses being smashed, the whole shebang.'

'What did you do?'

'Backup wasn't far away, so I thought I'd get the dog out and make a start. I opened the van doors, then the cage door and gave him the order to jump out.'

'And . . . ?' I was on the edge of my seat.

'Nothing. He lay there, stretched his legs out, looked at me, yawned and put his head back down on the bed.'

'Wow!' I said. Yawning can be a sign of stress in dogs and I didn't expect a police-trained Rottweiler to turn out to be a scaredy cat. I asked the obvious question, obvious to me at least. 'Was he nervous?'

'Nervous? Hell, no. He's too chilled out for that. He wanted a nap. He wasn't the slightest bit bothered about the fight. He was, like, "Oh, let them kill themselves, Dad, we're OK." If someone had come round the back of the van and hit me, he'd have been there like a shot and nailed them, but for the time being he couldn't be bothered working and he was happy in his bed.'

'So, he wasn't nervous, he was calm?' Stating the obvious seemed risky, but I wanted to be clear.

'Calm . . . ? He was calmer than me. I was bloody livid! Especially when three other bobbies turned up – nice of them to join the party – and asked why I hadn't got the dog out yet.' He paused. 'Anyway, that was the last straw. He'll never make a police dog as long as he's got a hole in his arse.'

So, calmness is a bad thing? Well, not quite. It's only in certain circumstances that too much calmness is bad. More often than not – and particularly with pet dogs – calmness is a much better choice than too much excitement. It's a case of horses for courses. To illustrate the point, when I ran seminars I asked audiences to shout out what problems they thought dog owners had when they called me for help. I asked for guesses as to the top five. The fact is that I hadn't run the numbers and I didn't actually know what the top ones were (although I could have guessed them pretty accurately). The running order wasn't as important as what we perceive dog behaviour problems to be.

The answers would come in thick and fast, almost too quickly to scribble on the board. Aggression, barking at passers-by, pulling on the lead, separation anxiety, destructive behaviour, attention seeking. I'd call a stop after a minute or two and confess that actually I didn't exactly know which were the top five and that, to some extent, it was irrelevant because the stats would change from month to month. But I then asked if they could see any similarity in the problem behaviours they'd listed. Although they always appeared very disparate, to me there was always one obvious common denominator. At least it's obvious once you've seen it.

Sometimes, I'd offer a clue. 'Would you describe these issues as too calm or too excited, do you think?' It's a lovely thing to watch the faces in an audience turning one by one from bemused to enlightened in a happy contagion. 'Too excited!' people would say, excitedly. Others would nod, fold their arms and sit back in a satisfied, wry-smiling, I-get-it kind of way. Sometimes I'd throw a spanner in the works. 'But what about separation anxiety? Or any anxiety for that matter? Is that really excitement?'

The answer becomes easier when you turn the question on its head (that's something I do a lot, incidentally). Instead of asking: 'Is anxiety excitement?' we might ask: 'Is an anxious dog calm?' The answer becomes way clearer. She's anything but calm when she's stuck in a whirlwind of horrible, can't-sit-still anxiety. Anxiety, and virtually any other common pet behaviour problem you can think of, is characterised by too much excitement.

The more you think of it, the clearer you see it. It's something I spotted early in my dog training career and, more than a decade later, having worked with thousands of dogs, I haven't changed my mind. In almost all cases, one thing holds true: excitement is the problem.

There's nothing wrong with a little excitement at the right

time, but too much at the wrong time is going to land you in a world of trouble. In the tens of thousands of enquiries we've had at Dogfather Training over the years, nobody has ever, ever called and asked, 'Please can you get Graeme to come quickly? You see, my dog's really calm.'

As we all knew all along, calm is a very good thing indeed.

If excitement is the root of all evil, why is it that dog trainers default to the 'whoopee-doo' approach so often? The answer is complex. Certainly, excitement is often at the root of a lot of the behavioural problems I see, but that's not to say that you won't want your pet dog to be excited sometimes. Getting a dog to come flying back to you on command, happily and quickly, certainly relies on a degree of excitement.

That said, if the premise you've been taught is, 'You must be the most interesting thing in the park,' then you'll be setting yourself up to fail because, sooner or later, something will always be more interesting than you. You simply cannot be the most interesting thing in the park 100 per cent of the time. Even with a pocket full of smelly treats, for many dogs the sight of a squirrel or another dog, perhaps a friendly human, will have him thinking: 'Yeah, yeah, Dad, you've got treats. But not now. I'll be there in a minute.' Incidentally, if you've never seen a 50kg Rottweiler, full of optimism, trying to follow a squirrel up a tree, I highly recommend it as a cure for the blues.

We've seen quite a lot of rev-them-up-to-the-high-heavens dog training. I have a theory about why that is. Many dog trainers traditionally came from a competition or professional background. I think we all know an ex-police dog handler who does a bit of pet dog training, or a former competition champion in obedience, agility or dog shows who now runs classes. To be successful, they were taught to rev their dogs up. In fairness – and credit where it's due – it worked well for them and presumably it seemed sensible to pass that excitement-based approach on to pet dog owners.

On the face of it, that's perfectly reasonable, but it's missing an important point. Compared to most competition or working dogs, the needs of pet dogs are very different. Not only do they lead different lives, they're often bred differently, too.

We should perhaps challenge whether we need to make dogs quite so excited all the time to make them happy. At seminars, I often encourage attendees to shout out the first thing that pops into their heads when I ask them to visualise a happy dog. 'A waggy tail!' is almost invariably the first thing that's shouted out. That's an interesting one, because a wagging tail isn't always a sign of a happy dog.

Of course, there's the kind of wagging tail that's part and parcel of the funny dance your dog does when he hasn't seen you for a while, such as when you pop around the corner to the Co-op for milk and he acts as if you've been away for months. I call that the full body wag. It's happy, but excited-happy. On the other hand, I've lost count of the number of times that a confused client has told me their dog was wagging his tail before he bit someone. Tails that wag quickly aren't all happy, but they are always excited. We'll talk more about this in later chapters.

After a waggy tail, the answers vary but typically revolve around dogs frolicking around, running through the countryside or playing with other dogs and owners, barking even.

They're happy – no doubt about that – but excitedly so. In the English-speaking world at least, happy and excited are linked.

We all know dogs can be calm-happy, too (a contented dog stretching out on his bed after dinner springs to mind), but it's not usually the first thing that pops up when we're asked to imagine happy dogs.

In other countries, it's not like this. My quest for knowledge extended outside the UK and I attended a dog training event in Germany a few years ago with a couple of friends from the dog training club of which I was a member. At the time, I'd just started to ask my 'How would you describe a happy dog?' question at seminars back home, and this was a chance to ask people who knew more than me. The bonus feature, as it turned out, was that coming from a different culture can make quite a difference to your outlook.

Over dinner one night, I was the only Brit at a table of dog trainers from all over Europe. I decided I should ask the German guy running the show my favourite question of the moment. Bernt was a big man with chiselled features and hands like shovels. He was also Bavarian. Bavarians and Yorkshiremen have a lot in common: we have the best beer in our respective countries (that's a fact, by the way, not an opinion); we speak properly (unlike everyone else who has the misfortune of not being born in our regions); and we have an 'I like what I say, and I say what I like' streak a mile wide. Or maybe a kilometre. I should probably add at this stage, before you set pen to paper, dear reader, that we also have a self-effacing sense of humour and you shouldn't take everything we say seriously.

Bernt knew a lot about dogs and could be relied upon to give a straight answer to a straight question. I picked my time and fired away. 'What does a happy dog look like?' The whole table looked at me and then at Bernt. There was a pause, but not a long one. It doesn't take a Bavarian or a Yorkshireman long to form an opinion that he will stick with long after anyone else stops caring.

'Lying down,' he said.

Lying down. Blimey. I ran the idea around my head for a couple of seconds. I'd asked the question of perhaps a hundred people back home and I was pretty sure nobody had ever given that answer. If they had, it was a long way down the list after 'waggy tail'. I was aware the other dog trainers were now nodding, knowingly. What, exactly, was I missing here?

'Why lying down?' I asked.

'It's obvious!' said Bernt. It certainly wasn't obvious to me. 'If a dog is feeling anxious, he is unhappy. He is on his feet because he is ready to fight or flight. But if he is lying down, then he is happy.'

Genius. Didn't someone once say that any idiot can make something sound complicated but it takes a clever person to make it sound simple?

Apparently, it was obvious if you were German. Belgian, French or Dutch too, judging by the faces around the table. But to me this was new thinking. How had I not worked that one out for myself? To these guys, happy conjured up images of contented, not excited, dogs. The way I viewed dog training had changed for ever. We think we want excited dogs when often we don't. But we always want them to be content.

Guide dogs are calm. When you think about it, that's just as well. They have to be, to do their job of leading visually impaired people around. It's important they are steady and dependable. Unlike police drug-detection dogs, who are bonkers-excited when they are working, no one wants a hyperactive guide dog. Hyper-alert yes, because they need to be aware of what's around them and always to look out for possible dangers, but never hyperactive.

Being physically calm is only part of the story, though, and arguably only the tip of the iceberg. To process everything that's coming at them, assistance dogs need to stay calm so they can think clearly. It's the same for any working dog. Even police dogs need to keep a cool enough head to listen to commands, even – or especially – when mayhem is all around them.

In that respect, dogs are like humans. It's easy enough to think clearly and see things in perspective when we're sitting at home quietly; it's much more difficult, or even impossible, if we allow ourselves to get too wound up. There's a level of excitement, a threshold, past which we cease to think clearly. Push people past that limit and they act irrationally and make bad decisions. Road rage is a classic example of this.

Some people must stay calm under extreme pressure to do their jobs. Take surgeons, for example. I had a minor heart operation last year to fix a little defect that, it turns out, I'd had since birth. It took place while I was awake and under a local anaesthetic. As you can imagine, I was a little apprehensive but I took the view that, since I was going to be in the theatre during a live operation, I might as well view it as an opportunity that life had thrown me to experience something new and perhaps to learn something. We've all seen the TV programmes and so what I wanted to know was, are they as calm as they seem on the telly?

I'm happy to report that, yes, they are every bit as calm as you'd imagine – certainly, the team that worked on me. There's a palpable feeling of taking things steadily and keeping a lid on excitement that leads to everyone focusing, apparently effortlessly, on the job in hand. Even when something a little unexpected popped up, the only clue was a very matter-of-fact, 'Gosh, that's remarkable,' from the boss, followed by a quick reassessment of the best way to proceed. Then away they went.

There's no doubt the feeling of calm rubs off. I was massively reassured that I was in good hands. That's handy to know when you're looking at a live scan of the inside of your heart. The fact it was still beating was reassuring too. (In case you're wondering, despite being 'remarkably' defective, I made a remarkably complete and speedy recovery, thanks to everyone who looked after me.)

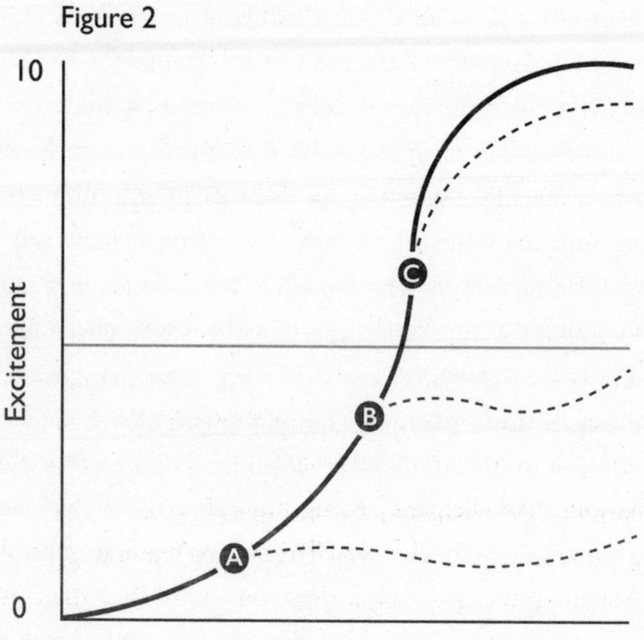

Keeping excitement at bay is key to being able to think clearly, whether you're a dog or a human. It's why managing excitement is the way to go when we're training our dogs. Rev them up too much and we take away their ability to think straight.

In figure 2 we can see the progression of excitement from 0 – a dog that is super-calm, dozing on its bed – rising to 10, which represents maximum excitement. The response is going to vary from dog to dog, but may include aggression, barking or even frozen-to-the-spot terrified. They're all different responses to out-of-control excitement.

Note the shape of the curve in figure 2. It's exponential – it climbs slowly at first but then accelerates rapidly, out of control, until it's almost a vertical line. If you can catch excitement early enough – as it starts to build (point A on the graph) – you may well be able to change the course of your dog's behaviour and calm her down.

If, however, you wait too long, you'll be fighting an uphill battle. The horizontal line is the threshold between being able to think clearly, and the red mist zone above the line where rational thought goes out of the window. Even if you were to try to stop the behaviour just before the threshold (point B), you may well find that you can't calm your dog for long enough to prevent her excitement immediately spiralling out of control again.

If you were to wait until she's on the steepest part of the curve (point C) it would be virtually impossible to make a dent in the behaviour. Like a helpless passenger in a car driven by a maniac, you can scream as much as you like, but you're not in control.

You may recognise in a dog you know that there is a point of no return, the moment they cross the threshold.

No amount of screaming and shouting, yanking on a lead or anything else you try will work. You'd have to try some really quite brutal stuff to make an impact on the behaviour of some dogs – and that absolutely is not what I'm about.

There are no brownie points for 'bigging it up' and trying to control a dog that's already too far over the line. It's far better to put yourself and your dog in a position where you can both stay calmer and clearer-headed instead. That's why my aim – wherever possible – is to operate under the line. Less drama makes for more effective learning.

A quick word about the steepness of the curve and the height of the threshold. Both vary from dog to dog. Steady dogs that are calm by nature and rarely fazed by anything will have a much higher threshold than nervous dogs that are constantly on edge. They'll also have a much less steep curve because it takes them longer to get excited.

In contrast, an anxious and flighty dog who has just found her forever home may be reactive to many things in the first weeks at her new place. The slightest noise outside, or anyone approaching the house, may set her off barking, for example. Not only does her excitement build more quickly (the steepness of the curve), but her threshold may well be lower too, which, in turn, means it's much harder for her to think clearly. The end result is that she panics readily and in response to things other dogs take in their stride.

The good news is that the shape of the curve and the threshold can change over time. As our scared dog gets used to the environment, and with the right input from her owners, she becomes steadier and able to cope more easily. To a large extent, this book is about flattening excitement curves and moving thresholds further up the graph. In other words, we're aiming for calmer and happier dogs.

So far, so good, but this is all great theory and it's missing an important point. Figure 2 assumes that we're starting at zero when, in fact, we rarely are. In the real world, it's a very rare dog (or person, for that matter) who spends their life trending at an excitement level of 0. Most of us spend our time between 1 or 2 and somewhere just under our threshold, with occasional bouts of losing the plot above it. Some of us spend way more than the average time above the line. If you've ever worked with someone like that, you'll know how stressed they are – and how stressed you become as a result. Just as with dogs, there's often a knock-on effect. Stressy owners equal stressy dogs quite often, and vice versa.

There's a phrase that pops up quite frequently in conversations with dog owners. It's on my 'wish I had a pound for every time I'd heard that' list. It starts like this: 'The problem with my dog is there's no time to react' – and here's the golden line that's going to make me a millionaire when all my wishes come true: 'because he goes from nought to a hundred miles an hour in no time at all.' If you have a so-called nought-to-a-hundred dog, or know someone who does, what I'm about to say next may come as something of a surprise.

It's not nought to a hundred in no time. It's an illusion. It's not nought to a hundred miles an hour at all (i.e. 0 to 10 on our graph). It may have ended up at a hundred, but while you weren't looking he was gradually winding himself up. Thirty, forty, fifty . . . the excitement crept up while no one was paying attention. Sixty, seventy . . . By the time you spotted it, it was far too late. No time to stop, he's way over the top. He was never at zero in the first place. He was probably over his threshold before you even became conscious of it. Eighty to a hundred in no time is nearer the mark. But that's great news, because between zero and eighty there's a lot of scope for us to change what we do, to prevent the crash in future.

To see how excitement creeps up on us, let's look at an example of what happens to a dog as his owner gets ready to take him for a walk. This plays out as we plot excitement on a graph, in figure 2. It's a very common scenario and I'd say that most dog walks start a little bit this way. What follows is a true story, but I've changed the names to protect an innocent dog and his well-meaning owner.

Vlad, the Romanian rescue, is chilling out on his comfy Barbour quilted bed in the sitting room of the house where his loving owners have given him a home for life. Vlad loves his new place. How lucky can a dog be? It's all a far cry from the way his life started. He's such a good boy in the house – but outside, it's a different story.

Little is known of his life before he was rescued in Bucharest, but we do know he was found wandering the streets, emaciated and fending for himself. He's not too keen on visitors to the house, but he tolerates them. The biggest problem is that, although he loves going for a walk, he reacts badly to many dogs and particularly to any that startle him. Perhaps he was attacked by dogs when he was stray – we'll never know. The fact is, if he's outside, he's on his guard.

Vlad's owner, Peter, puts down the *Guardian*, looks at his watch and stands up. 'Come on then,' he says, and walks to the hallway. Vlad doesn't need to be asked twice. He knows the signs. While he was snuggling on his bed, Vlad's excitement level was at one out of ten. Now it looks like a walk is on the cards and it rises to two. Peter picks up the lead. 'Yay!' thinks Vlad (in doggy Romanian, obviously). Peter gets down to dog level to attach the harness and Vlad backs up the hallway, tail wagging in excitement. This is point A on the graph.

He's not scared of the harness, but it's such a great game to see a 60-something retired teacher skedaddling along on hands and knees. Who said dogs don't have a sense of humour, eh? By the time it's all fitted, Vlad's shot through three on the excitement scale and he's easily a four. Peter faffs about with his coat, checks the pockets for treats and . . . oh, hang on, no poo bags.

A quick trip to the kitchen sees his dog wind himself up to a solid five and by now we're at point B on the graph. Peter comes back, stuffing the poo bags in his pocket. Tennis ball, ball flinger. Vlad is at five and a half. Peter's hand reaches for the door handle. 'Come on then!' he exclaims. 'Walkies!' Why do some dog owners shout, 'Walkies!' like this? The last thing you need before you start a walk is more excitement.

It's the last straw. Vlad is beside himself with anticipation, jumping around, barging past Peter's legs as he opens the door. One man and his dog walk out the door of the bay-fronted Victorian terraced house. The front garden is just six feet long. There's a brick wall and a creaky wrought-iron gate separating it from the pavement. It's a perfectly normal scene: Peter is as calm as ever and Vlad . . . Well, Vlad's as excited as ever. Five minutes ago, he was at level 1. Not now: he's racing up the graph at 6 and rising, just below his personal threshold of 7. A time bomb with teeth. Point three. Peter, of course, is blissfully unaware as he prepares for his walk to the park.

Sadly for everyone concerned, and despite all appearances thus far, this is not going to be a normal day. Walking along the pavement, way out in front of her owner, is Betsy the Pomeranian, a cute little happy-go-lucky ball of white fluff. Behind the brick wall, she's invisible to Peter, his hand now on the latch of the gate. Circumstances have conspired to put her on a perfectly timed collision course with Vlad. Betsy has no idea what is about to hit her.

Vlad explodes past his owner, with inevitable and shocking consequences.

As horrifying as the incident was, it could have ended so much worse. Betsy needed vet treatment for what turned out to be a superficial wound (Peter had managed to pull Vlad back as he momentarily let go of poor Betsy for a re-bite). Following an uncomfortably large bill and an excruciating police investigation, Vlad was given a stay of execution.

It was soon afterwards that I got the call to help. 'The thing is,' said Peter, once we were installed in his sitting room with a cup of tea, 'Vlad's completely unpredictable. One minute he's perfectly happy, the next minute ... bang! There's absolutely no way you can see it coming.'

It sounded familiar. 'It feels like nought to a hundred in no time ... ?' I suggested.

'Exactly!'

Clearly, we had a lot of work to do with Vlad and – more to the point – with Peter. A very good place to start is for owners to be aware of their dog's level of excitement at all times. You don't have to be obsessed with it but, like being aware of the speed you're driving when in a car, it's essential information. Arguably it's easier in a car because there's a speedometer in front of you; to judge your dog's excitement, you'll need to learn how to read their body language. It's not terribly hard and I'll help you with that later.

Incidentally, when I used to train new dog trainers, a question I often asked them was: 'How close do you think this dog is to the threshold right now?' The correct answer was ususally, 'Too close for comfort.' It's a good question, and one you should be asking yourself frequently.

Chapter 11
Time is your friend

'Don't run before you can walk' is good advice that I made a point of ignoring for most of my life. I'm impatient. It's just the way I am with most things. Except dog training.

We're constantly told that on-demand streaming TV, smartphones and instant online shopping are conspiring to create an anxious, I-want-it-now generation. I'm not so sure. Before that, the argument was that video rentals would kill off cinema and recording your own cassette tapes and playing them back whenever you wanted would spell the end of the music industry.

I'm just not buying it. Although I wasn't quite born impatient – I arrived two weeks late – I've been catching up ever since. I can't blame iPhones or internal combustion engines. Impatient is just the way I am. Actually, I think most of us are to some extent, particularly men. Patience, according to my grandma, was found seldom in a woman and never in a man.

I suspect it was ever thus. The first caveman who set himself alight by accident was probably told by an older cave-person (perhaps his cave-grandmother?) that no good would come of inventing fire and he should stop getting too far ahead of himself immediately and sit down with a nice cup of water because tea, of course, had not yet been invented.

So it was with me. Newly qualified, I took to driving like my hero, the rally champion Pentti Arikkala, whose Vauxhall Chevette was just like my grandmother's showroom-fresh GLS model, except that Grandma's had a pushbutton FM radio and chrome wheel trims, which Arikkala's clearly lacked. I lacked any rally driver skills whatsoever. Luckily (for it was luck, and not judgement), the car survived long enough for me to buy my own, an MG Midget, which I promptly crashed.

It was the same with ballroom dancing, decades later. In a triumph of enthusiasm over ability, I threw myself into it, quickstepping before I could slow foxtrot. As much as I fancied myself as Fred Astaire, I probably looked more like Farmer Giles waltzing in wellies across a field. Certainly, competition judges seemed to think so. It was a shame for my long-suffering dance partner, Lin. Her Ginger was always better than my Fred.

It wasn't until I got a Rottweiler for the first time that everything changed. I realised I had one chance to get it right. A Rottie was, after all, a serious proposition, and if I didn't know much about dog training when I got him (I didn't), then I'd better learn.

I threw myself into dog training at a club where I was lucky to meet some brilliant trainers. They were all keen amateurs, but only in the sense that they weren't paid; in everything else, they were professional. Every week I'd want to move on faster and every week I was told not to run before I could walk. It was sound advice and, since I was so determined to do a good job of bringing up two well-behaved dogs, for the first time in my life, I listened.

With training a dog, time is your friend. We all – dogs included – learn gradually. If we push too hard, things usually come crashing down, along with our confidence. Learning to drive isn't dissimilar. We usually learn the basics somewhere quiet and only when it's deemed that we're ready do we move up to tackle more difficult situations.

My first time behind the wheel was with my dad on the derelict runway of a former RAF airfield in Yorkshire. Not only was it quiet (possibly too quiet, since we perhaps weren't meant to be there), but there was enough run-off for a Halifax bomber. Or indeed for a Cavalier 1600 if the teenage driver had delusions of motorsport grandeur.

If you drive, it's worth remembering the uneasy, out-of-depth feeling you experience when being pushed to the next level. Done skilfully by an instructor who knows when you're ready, it's fine. It's part of the process of learning. Tackling a city centre at rush hour is not for the faint-hearted, however, and it certainly isn't lesson two material. We almost all get there in the end, but it takes time. Progression isn't linear, either. Just as with dog training, there are good and bad days; two steps forward, one step back. The trick is to create more of the good days by progressing steadily.

If you run before you can properly walk, you'll push your dog's excitement level beyond his calm-thinking threshold – and perhaps yours with it. It is the out-of-control excitement and the attendant lack of clear thinking that leads to a crash.

I recently had a call from a chap I'd seen not long before with his Border collie. Sky was quite a handful, barking and lunging at most other dogs around. We walked around the park together and it went really well. She wasn't perfect, but she was certainly much better than normal: 'This is the best walk we've ever had,' was the verdict from the client.

I had called time on the park walk after half an hour because I could see that it was beginning to be too much for Sky. Her excitement was building and she'd had enough.

Learning something – especially if it's in an environment that makes us anxious or stressed – is taxing. Sooner or later, dogs and people hit a limit where their ability to think clearly goes out of the window. The secret to building success is to stop while you're ahead. Bank the good behaviour every time and leave your dog with a series of behaviour-changing good memories.

'It was as good as gold with you,' said my client, when he called. 'But as soon as you went, everything started going downhill. It's like it was showing off when you were here. Waste of money.'

It! I hate people calling their dog 'it' with a passion.
I was concerned and surprised, not least for the poor dog. Dogs, even clever ones like collies, don't show off in the evil genius way he was suggesting. There had to be a simpler reason. I checked the notes I'd made during the consultation: *V. reactive. Improving.* That tallied with my memory. Then something jumped out at me from the bottom of the page. The very last thing I'd written, in quotation marks (which is my shorthand for something I'd advised in so many words) was a massive clue: 'Slowly does it.'

'When did it start to go wrong?' I asked

'Straight away,' said the man. 'Because it had gone so well,

I thought I'd go straight back out after you left and find as many dogs as I could. To practise. So, we walked around the park for a couple of hours but it just got worse and worse. It was off its head. Hasn't been the same since.'

I didn't know whether to laugh or cry. What part of 'slowly does it' had he not understood? I took a deep breath and embarked on a clearer and simpler definition. I'd made a schoolboy error: there are two syllables in 'slowly'. Sadly, that's one syllable too many for some folk.

Chapter 12
Leadership – who is leading who?

'Oh, sorry, Graeme,' my client interrupted me, mid-sentence. 'I just have to take him out.'

Jeanette gestured at her dog Benny, a chocolate-coloured working cocker spaniel at her feet. He was as bright as a button, like many of his kind, and cheeky. He knew what he wanted and how to get it by deploying his secret weapon: cuteness. 'I think he needs to go to the toilet.'

I was sure he didn't. For a start, he'd been only 15 minutes earlier. He wanted to go and play in the garden and for us to follow him. It wasn't a mystical ability to read dogs' minds that brought me to this realisation, more a knack for reading their body language. His whole-body wagging and his bright eyes screamed out: 'Play with me!' Also, it was the third time he'd pulled this particular stunt in the last hour. On the previous two occasions – disappointed that we'd not followed him – he had sat persistently tapping at the glass of the French windows to be let back in. The scratched glass bore witness to this bad habit.

'I might be wrong,' I ventured, 'but I'm pretty sure he doesn't need to go to the loo. How long can he hold it for normally, would you say?'

'Oh, for hours. Maybe eight hours if he really had to, I suppose.' Jeanette paused. 'He never goes to the loo in the night.'

'So, he can hold it for eight hours, but you think you have to get to the door in, what, eight seconds?' I smiled. There's a fine line between being patronising and pointing out something in a clear but kind way. Humour helps. 'I know he's cute,' I said, 'but I think he's wrapping you around his little finger.'

'I'm too soft with him. I can't help it. He's soooo cute.' Jeanette's eyes didn't move once from Benny as she spoke. He was cute – there was no doubt about that – and it is hard to ignore a cute dog. You'd have to be pretty hard-hearted to be immune.

Dogs know that cute works for them, or at least the clever ones do. In Moscow, it is estimated there are between 25,000 and 35,000 stray dogs that have learned surprising strategies to survive. Clearly, that's a lot of dogs, often organised in packs, roaming the streets of a very populous city. It sounds like a recipe for disaster, doesn't it? We might expect Muscovites to be frightened of the dogs. In fact, that's not generally the case because, largely, the dogs aren't frightening at all. Most have learned to co-exist with people and, as a result, are well tolerated or even liked by the city's inhabitants.

As well as learning to ride the subway trains and cross busy streets at pedestrian crossings – seemingly understanding the Walk/Don't Walk signs as they go – many of the capital's savvy street dogs have learned that being nice to people is the key to getting food. Being aggressive or even just nudging people simply isn't as effective. Humans don't like pushy dogs or people. Show us a cute dog, though, and most of us are big softies.

The strategy seems to have worked because Moscow's streets dogs are rarely underweight. On the contrary, they can afford to be picky because it's not hard to get food. It's interesting that the leaders of these groups of dogs are usually not the most physically powerful. This is a world where survival of the fittest has given way to survival of the smartest, according to biologist Andrei Poyarkov of the A.N. Severtsov Institute of Ecology and Evolution in south-west Moscow, who has studied the dogs for decades.

Followers take their lead from clever individuals. The same principle applies to pet dogs – and Benny was no exception. Like many pet dogs, he knew exactly how to get what he wanted. He was smart.

'The problem with Benny is that he doesn't listen to me,' Jeanette explained. 'One word from me and he does whatever he wants,' she laughed, 'My kids are way better behaved than him.'

It struck me as an interesting comparison. 'Out of interest,' I asked, 'what would you say to your kids if one of them asked for something with, "I want . . . ?"'

'Oh.' Jeanette scowled. 'That's just bad manners. There's a rule in our house: I want never gets.'

'Oh, I remember that one,' I said. 'I must have heard it a thousand times when I was growing up!' It probably says a lot more about me than my mum. 'So, here's the thing,' I continued. 'Imagine Benny was saying: "You! Woman! I want something!" I'm sure you'd think of it differently. He's not actually being quite so rude, but the end result is the same. He's telling you what to do. And you're doing it.' I looked at Jeanette to check she was following. 'So, imagine that it's happening for lots of different things: feed me, play with me, give me more room on the sofa . . .'

'Oh, tell me about it,' Jeanette jumped in. 'The other day I ended up sitting on the floor because he'd stretched out in the chair and there was no room for me.'

We both laughed. It is funny, but it has consequences, too.

'So, let's say he tells you what to do – and you do it – 15 times in a day. That's probably a conservative estimate. At some point, you ask him to do something and – guess what – he's thinking, "Er . . . I don't think so. I think you'll find I call the shots around here."'

'I've created a spoilt child, haven't I?' said Jeanette. 'I don't have spoilt kids, but I've spoilt the dog instead.'

It was a reasonable description of what had happened. Benny's crafty requests amounted to him taking the lead, while Jeanette's desire to give him what he wanted placed her in a 'follower' role.

If you have a similar issue, to turn the tables in a nice way is very easy. Of course, you'll still be letting him out to the loo, playing with him, feeding him and all the other things we do with our dogs, but you should be doing it on your terms. Like a parent saying to a child, 'Wait a moment, darling, I'm busy. I'll get to you in a moment,' don't jump to things straight away, and definitely don't reward your dog by getting out of your seat, throwing the ball or whatever he's demanding. As well as encouraging him to pester, you'll be chipping away at his view of you as the leader.

The same applies outside. If you're walking on your terms, you'll want to be deciding where to go, not him (vary it too, and keep him guessing – you're the one who knows where you're going next). You can decide when it's time to play and sniff – time to have a break, in effect – and when it's time to walk without stopping at every lamppost. Some lead, others follow. Take the initiative.

There's a great question that you can ask yourself whenever you're interacting with a dog. You'll know the answer instantly. It's something I think everyone should check many times a day:

Right now, who is LEADING this activity and who is FOLLOWING?

Any time you're interacting with your dog, you're either a leader or a follower. There's nothing in between and you certainly can't be both things at once. Be aware, also, that it can flip-flop very quickly.

Let's look at a quick example. A man walks to the kitchen and calls Einstein, his dog, who comes skedaddling in. Give yourself a gold star for leadership, man. You led and your dog followed. Hurrah! But what's this? As our man turns to the cupboard where the treats are, Einstein taps his leg. Having got Dad's attention, he lifts a paw. 'Oh, clever boy!' shouts the man (he got that right) and throws Einstein a tasty morsel. Who's leading who now? It had all been going swimmingly, too. Obviously, if the dog is demanding something of you and you follow on by giving it to him, you'd be kidding yourself if you think you're the leader.

You don't get to be in charge by being stronger or by shouting and screaming. Leadership isn't a euphemism for bullying, which will only make your dog unhappy, and still won't be effective at getting him to follow you to the ends of the earth. For that, try being kind and smart instead. I think of leadership as creating conditions for dogs (or people) to want to follow you, happily and willingly. You don't need to be powerful, but you do need to be a step ahead.

Keep asking yourself: who is leading and who is following?

* * *

What makes a good leader? Who was the best boss you ever worked for? Or the best teacher at school? Do you have a clear image of someone in mind? Hold that thought, because we'll be coming back to those people.

One Sunday evening in 2007, I was travelling home from the dog training club in Birmingham where I'd been volunteering, learning as much as I could about dogs and dog people. It had been a long day and, with my Rottweilers, Axel and Gordon, safely stowed in the back of my scruffy 20-odd-year-old Defender, I headed home down the M6.

My mind wandered and I was thinking about a couple of bosses I'd known when I worked in factories. Some weren't so pleasant to work for (least said the better), but a couple were really good. I was pondering the difference between the good and the bad. Good bosses don't need to scream and shout to get things done, for a start. They are nice to be around, and yet you wouldn't want to get the wrong side of them. The funny thing is that the very best have that about them, but no one has actually seen the 'other side'. You just know you don't want to go there – and you know how to avoid it.

They are consistent, too, which means that you know where you stand. That's a good feeling. They know how they like things done and how they don't. It creates an 'I know what you want from me' feeling. They reward good behaviour – and yet they never overdo it, I realised. Recognition means something and it creates an impulse to do more.

Another aspect, I decided, was calmness under pressure. The works manager uppermost in my mind was not known for his Zen-like nature, but in a crisis, instead of losing his head he'd pause, calm himself down and think. It had a positive effect on all around him. One last thing: they can be stubborn. Once they get an idea in their heads, not much stops them.

As we trundled along in the slow lane, I became aware that Axel had stood up and, through the dog guard, was breathing hot and heavy on the back of my neck. I knew it was him from the sound of his breath. It was early August and a sticky heatwave was making the journey uncomfortable. There are a lot of big lumps of metal in a Land Rover. The engine, gearbox, transfer box and axles are all full of hot oil, acting like radiators that never switch off. They are separated from the driver by a thin sheet of aluminium. Only posh Defenders have air con and mine was more dog van workhorse than Chelsea showboat. It had a radio – inaudible with the engine on – but that was pretty much its only refinement. (For the sake of clarity, there was plenty of airflow and the dogs weren't in any way adversely affected.) What it had in bucket loads was charisma, which meant I'd forgive it anything, including the pneumatic-drill-in-a-sauna sensory experience that it offered at that moment. Hot, sticky dog breath wasn't what I needed, but Axel had decided he needed a little air, too – and who could blame him? I didn't have the heart to shout over the din for him to lie down.

It was at that moment, with Axel reminding me of his presence, that I made a connection I've never forgotten. Here, behind me, was the dog equivalent of a good boss. My two dogs got on well – they were the best of chums – but there was never any doubt who was in charge. Axel led, Gordon followed. He could control Gordon with just a look if he wanted, effortlessly. He rewarded good behaviour, too. When it suited him – but only when it suited him – he'd honour Gordon with a cuddle, the canine equivalent of a pat on the back. The more I thought about it, the more I saw similarities. Perhaps leadership was an animal instinct? Some are born with it, but others can learn. Some don't.

Have you ever met someone and instantly thought, 'I don't know who you are, but you're someone important'? Some people have an air about them. It's hard to define, but they just have it. Some dogs, too. I've walked into thousands of dog owners' homes over the years and I'm more convinced than ever that some dogs are born to lead.

This kind of thinking was – still is, to some extent – heresy. Anthropomorphism is the attribution of human characteristics to a god, animal or object. It's the top cardinal sin of dog trainers and behaviourists. 'Thou shalt not talk about dogs as though they were humans' is fair enough to some extent, because there are indeed grave dangers in assuming dogs are exactly like us. They are not.

The problem, as I see it, is that we dog trainers occasionally throw the baby out with the bathwater and reject any similarities that are suggested between the species. 'Dogs are dogs and people are people,' is how it often comes across, 'and never the twain shall meet.' To suggest there is no crossover at all is nonsense, frankly. In the same way that there are differences, there absolutely are similarities. The more we learn about dogs in scientific studies, the more we see them. A solid foundation for our understanding of dogs might be a working knowledge of how they are similar to us and how they are not. Leadership, I'm convinced, is where similarities do exist between dogs and people.

So, back to my question. Who was your best boss or best teacher? They weren't the one running around like the proverbial blue-bottomed fly, screaming at everyone and changing the goalposts every two minutes, were they? They weren't panicky and inconsistent, I imagine. They were the one you could come to when there was a big problem and they'd somehow know what to do or how to figure it out. They'd communicate directly and clearly and always act with kindness.

Call me a heretic, but I've always found that works rather well with dogs, too.

If you ask anyone who knows anything about dogs if consistency is important, the answer will be a resounding yes – from me too, I might add. (And yet if you try to find scientific evidence to support the assertion, you'll struggle. A quick Google search for 'consistency' and 'dog training' reveals hundreds of web pages telling us how important it is to be consistent, but very little else.)

I'm a big fan of myth-busting, where appropriate, because there are a lot of things that have been said about dogs for years which turn out not to be true (that dogs see in black and white is one), but with this one I'm going with the flow. For good reason, dog trainers have banged on about consistency since Lassie was a lass.

Dogs like it if we're predictable. We sometimes associate that word with being boring, but for dogs, consistency helps them understand us. Predictable is reassuring and clear and good leaders score highly on those qualities. Unfortunately, all too often we're inconsistent in the way we communicate, usually without realising it.

If you want to lead a dog to better behaviour (and why wouldn't you?), here are a few tips on consistency that will help make life easier for both of you:

Don't get creative with language

We're pretty good at language. Dogs, less so. We say things in different ways and we usually rephrase something if we think we haven't been understood. It makes sense with other people, but not with dogs. Dogs much prefer 'Sit!' to be 'sit', and not have to second-guess what new phrases like 'Siddown!' mean. That's way too complicated. Choose a set of commands and stick to them, rigidly. If you must repeat something because it didn't work first time, don't rephrase it because you'll make it harder for Fido to understand, not easier. Fido likes simple. Be more Fido.

Don't use the right word at the wrong time

I went to see a family with a Dogue de Bordeaux-cross once, a lovely big lump of a dog who, I was told, didn't listen to the lady of the house. I sat on the two-seater sofa in their cramped sitting room and he joined me.

'Bongo! Get off there,' she shouted. 'Down!'

He did as he was asked. Staying on the sofa, he lay down right across my legs, burying my notes in the process. He'd been taught that 'down' meant 'lie down', of course. No wonder he looked surprised when she started grabbing him by the collar to drag him off, poor lad.

'You see . . . ?' she said, exasperatedly. 'He doesn't listen.'

Oh, the irony! It's worth remembering that dogs take things literally. If you've labelled a behaviour such as lying down with the command 'down', then choose another word for each new behaviour and stick to it. In case you're wondering, I think the word 'off' works very nicely for this particular problem.

One hymn sheet to share? That'll do nicely

If there is more than one person in a family, you'll not be surprised to hear that ideally you all need to be using exactly the same commands for the right behaviours. Singing from the same hymn sheet, so to speak. It certainly helps a dog to understand if you all stick to the same commands. To help you achieve this gold standard, you might agree on the words you'll all use and write them down. Put your document somewhere prominent, like the fridge door or your family notice board. It's a really good thing to do when you first get a puppy or a new rescue dog.

Two hymn sheets, if you must. But don't share

I'm going to contradict myself now. There are times when two people might use two different sets of commands. Take, for example, the clients I once met where a Frenchman wanted to speak to the dog in his native language, but his South African wife preferred Afrikaans. The obvious compromise was English. That's how we were conducting the consultation, after all, but there was a problem. While her parents, who visited a couple of times a year, spoke English as well as Afrikaans, his family didn't speak a word of English, only French.

'Our kids are tri-lingual,' they said. 'Can't we teach our dog to at least speak two languages?'

I get thrown some great challenges and while my knee-jerk reaction was to say, 'No way!' I thought again. The answer, perhaps surprisingly, is that yes, it is possible for two people to have different sets of dog training commands, but there's a catch. Both owners must stick exclusively to their own commands, not mix and match. Dogs are quite smart enough to understand that Dad has one way to say 'fetch' and Mum, another – two parallel streams of consistency, we might say. It takes longer to train (because there's twice as much for him to learn), but it is possible. The key is for each person to be absolutely consistent within themselves to avoid confusion, and to choose words which sound unique because, if the Afrikaans word for 'sit' happened to sound like the French word for 'down', there's an obvious problem.

Routines are good. And bad

Dogs like routines. Having a set routine before you leave for work, for example, can signal to your dog that they can settle down now because you won't be home for a while. By consistently doing the same things (which may include a few elements designed to settle your dog, such as nice long walk), you're helping him to understand what happens next. The same applies to bed time. The problem with routines is when they become a rod for our backs. Feed your dog on the dot of 5pm, for example, and it won't be long before he shouts the house down if you're running late. I prefer to feed in a window of a couple of hours, the same for walks, most days.

Chapter 13
How to read your dog

Understanding our dogs, knowing what they are thinking or what they are trying to communicate to us, is a fascination shared by most of us who are dog lovers. For many years, the most clicked-on part of the Dogfather website was an article entitled, 'What is my dog thinking?' That's perhaps surprising because there were always lots of practical articles on how to train a great recall or a nice lead walk – the bread and butter stuff of dog trainers – but the truth is we all want to know what's going on in our dogs' heads, too. Possibly more so.

I'm no more a mind reader than the next person, but I've learned over the years how to interpret what dogs are trying to tell us. Not speaking human language doesn't stop them sending out messages to us – and they're doing it most of the time. Much of it goes unnoticed or is misinterpreted because we weren't born – at least most of us – with an innate ability to understand the language of dogs, which is, of course, mainly non-vocal. Like any language, though, it can be learned.

Some seem to have a natural gift for it. I went to meet a family with a naughty yellow Labrador and a delightful little girl called Alice, who had a great affinity with her dog. As I chatted with her parents, she punctuated our conversation several times with dog status updates. 'Boo-Boo is bored!' she'd loudly announce, or 'Boo-Boo wants to go out.'

I began to realise that her pronouncements were not random; her reading of Boomerang (for that was his real name) were always spot-on accurate. Her ability to decipher the visual clues dogs use to communicate was amazing, especially for an eight-year-old. Alice was autistic, which may or may not be significant. I've found that many autistic people seem to really 'get' animals. I asked her what she especially liked about dogs. 'I like their earsies and pawsies and tailsies,' she announced, very sure of herself. She was impossibly cute.

'Earsies and pawsies and tailsies ...' I mused, as I rolled along the motorway a couple of hours later, homeward bound. I often mull over a meeting on my way back. I find it's quite often after the event that I realise I've learned something new: perhaps it's something I could have explained more clearly or something I heard someone say that I could borrow for another time. On this particular drive home, I had Alice's phrase ringing around in my head, like a catchy tune heard on breakfast radio that I end up, for the rest of the day, singing to myself (and to anyone else unlucky enough to be in earshot). Then it dawned on me: Alice was picking up a lot of what Boomerang was communicating to us – or at least trying to – by using his ears, his paws and his tail (plus, other body language cues).

If you'd asked me then to say which parts of dogs I look at when I'm reading them, I think I'd have placed the tail and perhaps the ears quite high on the list, but paws? Probably not. It was food for thought and, after a few years of reading countless scientific studies and working with thousands of dogs and their owners since, it's now clear that Alice was onto something. Paws do indeed send signals.

In this chapter, I'll look at a selection of dog body language signs and what they tell us about our dogs' thoughts and feelings. It's a subject that's worthy of a whole book (note to self). What follows isn't exhaustive, but is a combination of my experience, the tireless work of university researchers around the world, and the out-of-the-mouths-of-babes words of wisdom of an eight-year-old autistic girl. If Alice ever reads this book, wherever she is, I do hope she approves.

Earlier I referred to a dog eye-tracking study conducted in 2020 by the University of Lincoln. Research indicated dogs pay attention to the ears of other dogs, followed closely by their mouths and eyes, when assessing how the other might react to them. In contrast, when they look at humans, they target the frontalis first (the forehead muscle that controls frowns and eyebrow raising), followed by eyes, nose (because nostrils flare slightly when we're frightened) and cheeks (which flush, for various reasons). Many pet owners have sworn for years that dogs understand their facial expressions. Now the science is there to back it up.

The caveat is that we cannot be sure how well they understand the emotions behind our faces, although there are good indications that they have some grasp of it. For example, they're attracted to smiles, but wary of grumpy-looking people. One thing is clear: dogs absolutely recognise even tiny changes in our faces. So tiny, in fact (such as minutely flared nostrils), that they may actually be better at it than we are ourselves.

Logically, then, we'd expect them to be ninja masters at

facial recognition in their own species. So, who better to learn from than dogs themselves?

Since dogs focus on other dogs' ears first, they presumably apportion a high degree of importance – or urgency – to the information they glean there. That said, the fact they never look at one aspect in isolation also speaks volumes. There's always a bigger picture to look at.

The ears

Let's start with ears (a.k.a. 'earsies'). Our dogs' ancestors used their ears when hunting and protecting themselves from danger. Arguably, we're still seeing the effects of their heritage today. The first thing to note is that relaxed muscles are generally a good sign. It's something that is true for all aspects of a dog's body.

Canine ears vary a lot from breed to breed. Consider the difference between a German shepherd or a Westie, with their upright, pointy ears and, say, a basset hound, whose ears drape down the side of their face, halfway to the floor.

It's easier to talk about changes in ear posture if we consider pointy-eared dogs first, simply because it's so much more obvious. Broadly speaking, when dogs are alert, for whatever reason, the muscles controlling their ears tense and direct them, like little radar dishes, towards the source of the sound. 'Alert' covers a wide range of emotions from, 'Is that Daddy's car pulling up?' to, 'Is that the neighbourhood cat I've always wanted to chase?'

If looked at in isolation, many dogs' ears would look similar in both of these very different examples. What the rest of the face and body is doing is a huge clue to help us tell the difference. Alert ears with an excited 'whole-body' tail wag, an open-mouthed, lolling tongue and a bright-eyed happy expression is very different to 'target eyes' – snarling mouth and a locked-and-loaded forward stance. At the simplest level, upright, forward-pointed ears signal alertness or curiosity. But you'll need more than ears to understand the full story.

I think we've all seen a dog with alert ears tilting her head to one side or another in an effort seemingly to understand something we said. Sometimes they'll turn their head one way and then the other repeatedly. It's the kind of party trick that's spawned a thousand YouTube clips. What's really happening is that a dog is doing their best to listen more intently: 'If I turn this ear or that ear towards them, maybe I'll hear better and work out what they mean.'

The opposite of forward-pointing 'radar ears' are when they are flattened back against the head. In most cases, that's not going to be a good sign. Fear and nervousness springs to mind when I see it. Is the dog cowering? Does he look tense and ready to spring into flight or fight mode? He's clearly signalling: 'I'm not happy and I'm feeling on edge. I'm telling you not to push me.' Approach a dog like this at your peril.

I wish I had a pound for every time I heard the owner of a nervous dog tell me their worst nightmare is the local dog lover who insists that 'all dogs love me' and keeps trying to make friends despite the obvious protestations from their dog. It's tantamount to saying: 'You *will* love me, whether you like it or not.' Sadly, there's no telling them.

Sometimes, pulled-back doggy ears aren't a sign of full-on

fight or flight at all, but a halfway house. In the same way that curiosity can be halfway to alertness, there are times when folded ears are more a case of, 'I'm not sure about this.' Unease, rather than fear. Either way, tense muscles pulling ears backwards are likely to signal bad things, not good.

If your dog has hanging ears instead of pointy ones the same applies, but it's a little harder to spot. I lived with Rottweilers for many years and currently have a Labrador/boxer-cross. You'll never see one of those breeds prick their ears up to the extent you'll see it in a German shepherd, but the muscles still operate in the same way. The ears move forward and back, but to a less obvious extent. And the same principles still apply, even with dogs whose ears are heavy and dangly, such as spaniels and bassets.

If you know your dog, you'll soon learn the differences. It's trickier for professionals: we have to be instant experts (or as close as we can) with any dog we meet. As a dog owner, you only have to be expert in yours, however many you have. Given that they're already the world's leading authority on you that seems fair to me.

Incidentally, if you're interested in fearful dogs you might like to know that fight or flight is a little too simplistic a term. In nervous dogs, there are not two common responses but four. These are flight, fight, freeze or fawn; for more on this, see chapter 20.

The mouth

I've worked in lots of places but perhaps the most unusual, by my standards, was in a tropical rainforest in Queensland,

Australia in 2011. I rocked up in my hire car to a house in the middle of nowhere and was met by a very big German short-haired pointer called Stilts. This is not his real name but, like the house he lived underneath, he'd been built on a very long set of legs. Stilts came bounding up to the car before I'd even arrived at the house and ran around and around until I stopped. He then alternated between the passenger window and mine, pressing his face up to the glass and baring his teeth, eerily without making a sound.

'What do we do now?' asked my girlfriend, clearly more than a little perturbed.

'We get out,' I said, doing my best to sound sure of myself, 'because he's friendly.'

'You sure . . . ?' she asked

'Sure,' I replied.

I was 99 per cent sure (that qualifies, doesn't it?) because I'd read his expression and, although he was baring his teeth, his lips were relaxed and his tongue was hanging to one side, not drawn back ready to bite. (Top tip: if you can see a dog's tongue sticking out, it's usually a good sign. If he's going to bite, he will not want to impale his own tongue.) The rest of his body looked relaxed, too. This wasn't, I reasoned, a snarl. It was a smile. Here was a dog who loved people. Theoretically, at least, he was friendly.

Although I wasn't as experienced then as I now am, I knew enough, I thought. Putting to the back of my mind the 1 per cent lingering doubt, I smiled back at him and made moves to get out of the car. It turned out that's easier said than done when a big dog is trying to get in the same door to meet you halfway. I offered the back of my hand and was, I confess, ever so slightly relieved to see I was more in danger of being licked to death than bitten.

'See . . . ?' I said, brushing away any evidence that the 1 per cent doubt had ever existed. 'He's friendly.'

What I'd spotted was a submissive grin. Owners often describe it as a smile because the teeth are on show, and it looks very different to the threatening dog-baring-teeth click-bait stock image that tabloid newspapers roll out every time there's a dog attack story to cover.

You'll sometimes see submissive grins in 'dog shaming' internet videos. It's often paired with squinting eyes, a partially turned head and sometimes flattened ears. It's important that we don't slip into anthropomorphism here. Despite appearances, dogs aren't really 'sorry' in these videos because they don't understand what they've done wrong and why it's wrong. What many have learned to do, though, is to give us a cute, submissive grin in the hope we'll melt and everything can go back to normal.

What Stilts had learned to do – and it's relatively unusual with a stranger – was to meet people with a grin and hope that they'd be friendly. Visitors have a tendency not to be hostile in any case and so a self-fulfilling prophesy was born. 'I grin to make them friendly,' Stilts would tell himself, and they were. Fair dinkum.

'G'day!' A voice boomed out from the balcony above. My client, Shane, was a larger-than-life character. They don't do shrinking violets in Queensland – it's against the law. 'Don't worry about him,' he shouted down to me, waving at the now leaping-for-joy looney. 'He wouldn't hurt a fly.'

'No worries!' I shouted back, with an accent that sounded

part Aussie and part Yorkshireman. It earned me a disapproving look from my girlfriend. I'd been in Australia for all of a week and I was beginning to drop into the accent, quite unintentionally.

We went up the stairs to the house and Shane told me a little more about Stilts. 'He does that to everyone. He mobs them like a grinning idiot. Some people get it, but others are terrified of him. The other day I was out in the bush, about five kilometres away, and I got a call on my cell phone. It was a tradesman who'd arrived to give me a quote for some work. He said he was trapped in his Ute [pick-up truck] because the dog was snarling at him through the window and he couldn't get out. I told him it was fine, but he insisted on me coming back to save him from the scary dog.'

Grins are one way dogs communicate with us, but there are others. It's widely known that licking lips and yawning can be signs of stress, but it's only in recent years that researchers have understood how often dogs use these signs to tell us how they are feeling.

In a study published in 2018 in the journal *Behavioural Processes*, teams from the universities of São Paulo in Brazil and Lincoln in the UK found that dogs would lip-lick and yawn when they saw angry human faces. In itself, this doesn't sound entirely surprising, except for two further discoveries.

Firstly, regardless of whether the human faces came with a soundtrack of matching negative voices, the results were unchanged. It's more proof that dogs make their minds up about us from what they see, not what they hear.

Secondly, the study found that dogs lip-lick and yawn much more toward angry-looking humans than the equivalent images of dogs. That's perhaps surprising, and led the scientists to conclude that not only do dogs have a functional understanding of our displayed emotions, but also they may use displays of mouth-licking to facilitate dog–human communication.

Stilts had taken that concept and supercharged it. He wasn't about to wait for people to look angry before he gave them his goofy look. Oh no, he'd decided to give them the look first and wait for them to love him. As strategies go, it was a beaut, as they may or may not say in Queensland.

The eyes

If you've ever thought your dog was trying to tell you something when he gazes longingly into your eyes, you'd be right. It's not just wishful thinking that dogs communicate with their eyes (or at least attempt to, because the person at the receiving end may or may not understand). Scientific studies in recent years have proven that there's something special in the way dogs look at humans.

In a 2003 study carried out in Hungary, researchers trained dogs and wolves to access food in boxes and then ran an experiment to see what they would do when the boxes were made impossible to open. The wolves tried for a while, realised it was futile, and walked off (in a wolfy huff, presumably). The domestic dogs, however, hung around and looked back at their people with a long enquiring gaze, as if to say, 'C'mon, we're a team, open the box for me, would you?'

The result was all the more significant because the wolves were fully socialised with their handlers, having been raised by them since they were four-day-old puppies, and were brought up in family homes and a farm, then trained in the same way as the dogs.

Perhaps it's not surprising that thousands of years of domestication have created such different neural pathways in dogs' brains that even after a couple of years of training the wolves could not possibly imitate. For all the obvious similarities, dogs simply aren't wolves. Their ability to communicate with us using their eyes is perhaps unique in the animal kingdom. Sorry, cat lovers. I like them too, but there's a reason 'puppy-dog eyes' are just that, and not 'kitten-cat eyes'.

There's no denying that gazing into the eyes of a dog you love feels great. It's partly down to the hormone oxytocin, which is also known as 'the love hormone' for its role in early attachment between mothers and their babies, as well as the bonds between romantic partners. Oxytocin is rather special. It has been linked with promoting trust between individuals and protecting against fear and anxiety, as well as having an anti-inflammatory effect and preventing the premature ageing of muscle cells.

Animal behaviourist Takefumi Kikusui, from Azabu University in Sagamihara, Japan, conducted an intriguing experiment in 2008 to test whether interacting with dogs had an effect on oxytocin production. The results were astonishing.

Kikusui asked 30 pet dog owners to participate. He also tracked down owners of wolves, who were bringing them up as pets, and persuaded them to enter the experiment too, for comparison. Owners were asked to hang out with their animals for 30 minutes, during which time they talked to them (as you do), petted them and simply looked at them. Looking into each other's eyes was limited to short periods of up to two minutes (because staring is rude, as my mother always told me. It's the same between dogs. Also, don't stare at wolves. It's bad for you).

Of the owner/pet duos that had spent the most time gazing at each other, both male and female dogs experienced a 130 per cent rise in oxytocin levels, and their owners, both male and female, a 300 per cent increase. In contrast, no oxytocin increase was found in the wolves or in the dogs that didn't make eye contact with their owners.

If gazing produces oxytocin, Kikusui reasoned, it may work the other way around. Does increased oxytocin create more eye contact? A second experiment was devised in which dogs were given a nasal spray of oxytocin before interacting with their owners. No wolves were involved in this study. 'It would be very, very dangerous to give a nasal spray to a wolf,' Kikusui is reported to have said, wisely. The results were clear cut. Female dogs given the spray spent 150 per cent more time gazing at their owners, who in turn saw a 300 per cent increase in oxytocin levels. Interestingly, no effect was seen in male dogs. This makes some sense, considering the mother and baby bonding role played by the hormone.

Sadly, eye contact isn't always associated with good emotions. I describe the loving gaze as being characterised by soft eyes. The opposite effect is something I call target eyes, which happen when a dog locks onto something he's either intent on attacking or determined to run away from. Soft eyes are calm; target eyes are on high alert.

The closest human equivalent – although it's not an exact

match – is 'eyes like dinner plates'. We widen our eyes when we're surprised or scared. The biggest difference is that, while the whites of human eyes are always on show, for most dog breeds that's not true. If a wide-eyed dog isn't moving their head but is following your every move with their eyes, you'll often see the whites of their eyes, typically in a half-moon shape. The image I have in mind is a dog guarding a bone between his paws: head still, but eyes locked on as we move around the room. In a situation like this, seeing the whites of a dog's eyes is a sign that he's uncomfortable or anxious. The message here is clear: stay away!

* * *

Have you ever wondered what it's like to see the world through your dog's eyes? There are a few common misconceptions around about canine vision. The most enduring is that they see only in black and white, or rather, in shades of grey. In fact, it's been known for decades that they see colour, but not the full spectrum we do. The world for dogs is seen in tones of blue, greys and murky yellow. The range of reds and greens we see is perceived very differently by dogs. We might consider them to be red/green colour blind, in effect. Which is odd, considering one of the standout colours for dog toys is red. Standout to you and me, it may be, but not to Fido. If you've ever seen a dog struggle to find a red ball on a lawn, that's why. Red pops out against a green background to us, but it's more akin to camouflage for dogs.

Another common assumption is that dogs see better than we do. Certainly, their sense of smell is legendary and we know that they can hear things we can't, so surely they are in possession of similarly impressive eyesight? Well, yes and no, but mainly no. Their visual acuity (sharpness) in particular is woefully bad by human standards.

To understand quite how bad, we need a working knowledge of how eye tests are scored. The term 20/20 vision is familiar to most of us. It's a reference to the Snellen scale. Twenty refers to feet. The metric equivalent in metres is 6/6. Here's how it works: if you can see an image 20 feet away that a person with normal vision can see at 20 feet, you're said to have 20/20 vision.

However, if you are diagnosed with 20/40 vision, it means at 20 feet you can see the same detail a person with normal vision sees as far away as 40 feet. The minimum Snellen requirement to qualify for a driving licence in many countries, including the UK, is exactly that – 20/40 (6/12). That's corrected eyesight. (Is it just me, or is that a tiny bit worrying?)When dogs were tested, their normal eyesight acuity was measured at 20/75. Put simply, a dog can just make out something at 20 feet that a person with good eyesight can see at 75 feet, almost four times further away. It's quite a thought that guide dogs have such poor eyesight that, if they were human, they'd have to wear spectacles to pass a driving test, operate machinery or, presumably, guide a blind or visually impaired person around.

It begs the question: how on earth do they do such a good job? The answer is partly that they use their other, finely tuned senses to very good effect, but also that there are aspects of dogs' eyesight that make them as well suited to guiding a visually impaired person in an urban environment as catching a ball in the park or even hunting. And therein lies a clue.

In Germany in 1936, a chap called Schmid set out to

discover if dogs were better at seeing moving objects than stationary ones. He tested 14 police dogs and discovered they could recognise a moving object at up to 900 metres, but if the same object were presented not moving, the best they could do was 585 metres. That's quite a difference. Having eyesight with an in-built motion detector (and I'm including the processing system, the brain, in this), is essential to a predator.

Fast-forward to the 1970s and researchers looking at dogs' field of vision made an interesting discovery: when dogs look dead ahead, they can see things behind them. The shape of the skull has an effect, too, because short-faced breeds, such as pugs, see less well to the side, while the long and narrow skulls of breeds like greyhounds lend themselves to a wider view.

Humans see roughly 180 degrees, in front and to our sides. Try this little test for yourself: look straight ahead and, without moving your eyes, hold your arms straight out sideways and slowly move them forwards and backwards until you're able to assess where they disappear from view. For most of us, you'll struggle to see more than 160–180 degrees. The field of vision for a dog with an average-shaped head is closer to 240 degrees, which translates to an ability to see one third of everything behind them, that is from a line 180 degrees side to side, to their tails. And they can do this without moving their eyes from straight ahead.

None of this would be much use if the system didn't work in low-light conditions – when prey animals may come out of hiding. That ability is down to light-receiving cells in the eyes. Cone cells are good at picking up subtle differences in colour while rods cells operate much better at lower-light levels.

Humans have cone-dominant retinas, hence our extended colour range; dogs' retinas are rod-dominant and, as a result, their ability to see in low light is much better than ours.

For all their limitations, dogs' eyes and brains are finely tuned to spot things that move, across a wide field of vision and in low light. If we were talking about a CCTV system, we'd describe it as a wide-angle camera with inbuilt automatic motion detection and night vision. Not only does it equip dogs well for guarding or hunting, but also for spotting a London bus approaching the road you're about to cross, even if the bus is behind you and it's getting dark. Pretty cool, don't you think?

The tail

Ask most people how they might tell if a dog is happy and they'll probably mention a wagging tail. Although that's often right, as I pointed out earlier it's not always a sign that dogs are happy. A fast-wagging tail is an indicator of excitement, and that comes in various flavours. Happy is just one of them.

There's plenty of evidence that dogs use their tails to flag how they are feeling. We know from studies that, regardless of how happy dogs are, they don't wag their tails nearly as much when other dogs or people aren't around to see it.

It makes sense to use a tail as a highly visible signalling mechanism, a kind of doggy semaphore. Dogs' eyes and brains are fine-tuned to movement rather than high-definition detail. It's an essential attribute for a hunting predator – if it moves, it might be dinner. There's speculation among biologists that white and dark tail tips may even have evolved to improve visibility and help dogs communicate at a distance.

It gets better. Scientists have discovered that dogs' tails wag with a left or right bias – and they mean very different things. For the sake of clarity, by wagging to the left I'm referring to the dog's left, as seen through his eyes. If we're stood in front of him, a left-biased wag appears to the right as we see it.

Researchers at the University of Trento in Italy discovered in 2013 that when dogs observe other dogs wagging their tails to the right, their heart rates stay normal (or slows down) compared to seeing a non-wagging dog. In contrast, if they see a left-biased wag, heart rates rise and signs of anxiety and heightened alertness creep in. Dogs don't think wagging tails are at all good if they wag to the left, or the right as we see it.

The reason for this is that the left side of the brain controls the right side of the body and vice versa. So, a right-biased wag comes from the left brain, which is associated with positive emotions and 'approach behaviours'. In dog speak, 'I'm happy, let's get closer.' The opposite is true of a left wag, associated with withdrawal behaviour or, 'Back off!'

Here's my easy way to remember it: right is all right. Left is best left.

Check it out the next time you come home and your dog greets you at the door. Even though his tail will be wagging in big sweeps, with any luck you'll be able spot a right-side bias (left as you see it).

If you've never noticed before, take a moment to marvel at how much dogs pick up that we don't. You may never view a dog's tail in the same way again.

It's important we bear in mind that a normal tail carry varies considerably from one breed to another and from one individual to another. For example, a low, dangling, relaxed tail position that would be normal for some sight hounds would be very different for huskies and Akitas, with their tails curved up and over their backs, even when they are happily relaxed. Generally, though, for any given dog, a higher tail indicates alertness or excitement and a particularly low carry is unhappy, anxious, or fearful – especially when the tail is tucked underneath the body.

There are, of course, exceptions. Pointers will stop dead and indicate a bird ahead, out of sight, by stretching their nose out, lifting a paw and tensing their tail, rod-like, horizontally. When most other dogs are this alert, they'll have a tail bolt upright or curled up and over their back. So, it's important to know what's normal for your dog. If you don't already, get into a habit of checking their tail in many situations, including on a walk, and especially when you encounter other people and animals.

When I meet a dog I'm working with, I figure out what's normal for them as quickly as I can, often double-checking with owners. I use the dog's tail (and ears) as an instant barometer of progress. If I'm walking with a dog that is scared of the outdoors, I'll note her tail carry at the outset – tucked underneath, let's say – and I'll keep checking at different times. If we're walking away from traffic and her tail eases up towards a more neutral position, I'll make a mental note that, for example, traffic may be an issue. Being closer to traffic might be making an apparently unconnected problem worse, such as aggression to other dogs. That's because, like us, when dogs are already stressed, they can be more reactive. If we walk past a horse and rider and her tail stays relaxed, but then she hears a distant motorbike, I'll check her tail again. If it's dipped back down to 'scared', I'm getting useful information all the time.

Docked tails (those shortened surgically, often soon after birth) present something of a problem. Although docking tails for purely cosmetic reasons has been illegal in the UK since 2007, working dogs and pets imported from other countries are sometimes seen with docked tails. If other dogs can't easily see a tail, they're missing important information from the doggy semaphore, which could potentially lead to misunderstanding.

This makes sense in theory, but experience has taught me that it doesn't seem to be such a big deal in practice. I think perhaps it's because dogs take their cues from a wide range of body language signals, not just the tail. Also, we know tails aren't the first place dogs look when they're checking out other dogs. A missing tail must certainly be a hindrance to canine communication, but, as with most things in life, it's not a black and white issue. My own Rottweilers, Axel and Gordon, had docked tails. They lived to ten years old and in the thousands of interactions they had with other dogs in all those years, I can't remember once that a dog misread them to the extent it caused a problem.

Docked tails weren't my choice. It was very hard to find Rottie puppies with full tails before the ban, partly because breeders with any ambition to compete in Kennel Club shows were reluctant to field a dog with a tail because they were often marked down.

Some time after the ban came in, I was asked to judge a fun dog show. Luckily for me (since I know not the first thing about show judging), a 'proper' breed judge was on hand to help me with the conformation (Crufts-style) classes. She explained to me that she'd give second place to a Rottweiler who would have won his class but for a tail carry that was too high, a fault. She awarded top place to a dog that wasn't quite as good in some respects, but had a docked tail. I pointed out that if the winning dog had a full tail, he might have been 'faulty' too, but of course we couldn't tell. 'Exactly,' she said, 'if we can't see it, there's no reason to mark him down because he has no faults.' No wonder people who showed their dogs often took the view it was better to dock. There's a kind of logic there, but it always seemed wrong to me.

I entered Gordon in the waggiest tail competition at a fun dog show once. He won hands down. Or paws down, perhaps. The judge approached each contestant individually and timed ten seconds and counted the wags. Owners, meanwhile, did their frantic best to whip their dogs into a tail-wagging frenzy. It was hilarious to watch – the owners, of course, not the dogs. Gordon might not have had much of a tail (about an inch), but what he did have, unencumbered by the weight that slowed the other dogs down, didn't so much wag as vibrate. He was a happy chap at the best of times and it thrummed away so rapidly that the judge completely lost count. Result? Game, set and match to the scary 'devil dog.' He wasn't scary at all, of course, or a devil dog. He was a teddy bear (and they're only scary if you suffer from arkoudaphobia, possibly the most common affliction you've never heard of. Happy Googling!).

There's a twist to this tale. A little girl came up to me afterwards. She can't have been older than four or five and was impossibly cute. Her mum explained her daughter had a question for me and ushered her forward.

'Why doesn't Gordon have a tail?' she asked, in the blunt way that children ask great questions.

I paused, sensing that Mum was – not unreasonably – hoping for something suitable for little ears. The little girl eagerly awaited my answer. Her mum looked on, expectantly. With the benefit of hindsight, I now realise that, 'He was born like this,' would have been just fine. Short, to the point, and (importantly, I feel) avoiding any reference to two-day-old puppies being mutilated.

I could have said that, should have, but I didn't. 'Ah, well, you see,' I said, fumbling for something to say, 'it's just that . . .' and then it came to me. The perfect answer. 'One day when he was very happy he started to wag his tail. He wagged and he wagged and he wagged' – by now, I was beginning to fancy myself as a children's short story writer – 'and then he wagged some more, and then even more until' – it was all going swimmingly well – 'his tail fell off.'

'WHAT . . . !?' shrieked the girl and her mother in unison. The girl, clearly traumatised, burst into tears and refused to be consoled. It turns out that the idea that doggies' tails break off when they wag them is not the best image to put into an impressionable young child's mind. And if, by some bizarre quirk of the universe, you're reading this and recognise yourself as that young girl, let me take this opportunity to apologise for your lost childhood. I'm sorry. Really, I am. It was only meant to be a little white lie and obviously tails don't break off when they wag. Of course not. The truth is much more awful.

The paws

Just like humans, dogs can be left and right-handed. A 2016 study of pet dogs conducted at the University of Adelaide in Australia, reported that 34 per cent were left-pawed and 29 per cent were right-pawed, while 37 per cent of those tested showed no preference at all. They were, in fact, ambidextrous. Extrapolated, that means roughly one third of the dog population falls into each category.

With humans, the split is closer to 90 per cent right-handed and 10 per cent left-handed (estimates vary around the world). In the permissive Western world, the figures indicate slightly more left-handers than in parts of Asia, where children are more likely to be discouraged from favouring their left hands and where individuals identifying as left-handed may be as low as 3–5 per cent of the population.

Studies in humans over decades have indicated left-handers are more likely to be creative, have better verbal reasoning skills and, as a friend who is a proud 'leftie' reminded me recently, are more likely to rank as geniuses in IQ tests. He may have a point. He's smarter than me and can talk a good talk but, on the upside, I can buy cheap scissors and can openers, which goes some way to compensating for my inadequacies.

The obvious question this raises is do left- and right-pawed dogs (and ambidextrous ones) show different behaviour characteristics, too? The answer is yes and partly that's because, as we discovered with tails wagging one way or the other, the left-hand side of the body is controlled by the right side of the brain, and vice versa. But before we explore the implications, you may want to learn how to test your own dog and discover which of the three categories they fall into.

The method used in many scientific studies is the 'Kong™ test'. A rubber toy is filled with tasty food which, because it readily rolls around the floor, requires a steady paw to hold it still while the dog extracts the good stuff with her snout. Most dogs show a tendency to use either their left or right paw. The test needs to be repeated many times to arrive at a reliable conclusion. University studies take 50 paw holds to be the standard.

If you don't have a suitable toy to hand, hiding a treat or favourite ball just out of reach under a low piece of furniture such as a sofa will simulate the effect. Make a note of the paw your dog prefers to use to reach it.

Finally, a method which was verified in a PhD thesis by Dr Lisa Tomkins of the University of Sydney in 2010 is called the 'first-stepping test'. It couldn't be simpler and has proven more accurate and quicker that the Kong™ test favoured by most other studies. Wait until your dog is standing with both paws roughly level and when he steps off to walk, make a note of which leg he advances first. Using this method, 50 movements can be observed in 20 minutes. (Compare that to the four hours it takes in the lab to collect data for a Kong™ test.) If you're wondering how ambidextrous dogs show up in this, they'll tend to step off with either paw or if jumping up or down a step, will sometimes hop with both legs at the same time.

Dr Tomkins's studies focused particularly on guide dogs,

and she found right-pawed dogs were more likely to be successful in their training than those who were left-pawed or ambidextrous. More recent studies have indicated left-pawed dogs may show a slightly increased tendency to aggression towards strangers, and that ambidextrous dogs may be more prone to anxiety triggered by loud noises such as thunder and fireworks.

If you're thinking of using this information to help you choose your next puppy or rescue dog, please don't. There are many, many factors that affect dog behaviour and paw bias is only one. To say, 'Right-pawed, good; left-pawed and ambidextrous, bad,' is way too simplistic. I don't make a habit of assessing handedness when I'm meeting a dog I'm tasked with helping. It's interesting, for sure, but it's not a huge deal. I'll let you into a secret: I haven't even assessed my own dog, Lily. She is who she is, and I love her regardless.

For me, the main takeaway from this is there are more similarities in the way dogs and humans are wired than the prevailing wisdom had it when I started dog training. 'Dogs are dogs and humans are humans,' was the mantra. Of course, we're very different, but we're also quite alike – and it's the similarities that help us understand them.

Before we move away from paws, I'd like to say a little about the 'paw lift': when a dog stands still and lifts a front paw, waiting for something to happen. It often comes across as very cute because we associate it with the puppy game of shaking hands.

You'll see a paw lift happen spontaneously when there's anticipation in the air. In the same way that pointers and setters indicate with a raised front leg when they sense a bird ahead, many dogs paw-lift when they're taking a moment to check something out. Is that a cat under the hedge? Does Mum have a treat for me? Is that stranger friendly or not? Nothing screams out, 'Hang on a sec!' more than a dog lifting a paw. Want an easy way to remember it? Paws for thought.

Getting a puppy to do a handshake trick is the easiest bit of dog training you'll ever do, for that reason. If you think you've done an amazing job because your ten-week-old cockerpoo is shaking your hand on cue, I hate to burst your bubble but the truth is Mother Nature did most of the heavy lifting for you. Withholding a treat will often create an instinctive paw lift. Add a command like 'paw' and an outstretched hand of your own, reward with a treat (puppies are programmed to eat, after all) and you're there.

Call me a spoilsport, but while we're on the subject of teaching puppies to paw, I'm not terribly keen on it, especially with bigger dogs. It's fun when they're young, but not quite so amusing when they grow up and you're being batted on the leg constantly. Not to mention the inevitable day he runs full tilt through a muddy puddle to an unsuspecting passer-by wearing pristine white jeans and renders them camouflage. Hilarious. My top tip for teaching 'paw'? Don't.

Whole body-signalling

As with many things in life, it pays to look at the bigger picture with dog body language. Understanding what individual signals we might pick up by looking at a tail or ears, for example, is great, but it's limited. You'll understand far more by looking at the sum of the parts of your dog's body.

There are a few whole-body signals to watch out for which I think should be in every dog owners' knowledge bank and so I've included them here. It's a huge subject and space is limited so, with the usual caveat about non-exhaustive lists, let's start with the bad stuff and then we'll end this section on a positive.

When dogs are anxious or stressed, they stiffen up, just like humans. When I see a dog that was previously relaxed tense up, he's got my undivided attention. Something has made him ready to take action, whether it's to move forward or to back off (fight or flight). Tense is almost always bad news. In the same instant, his eyes will focus like lasers on whatever's bothering him. We've talked about eyes previously, and you'll find it easy to spot target eyes if you can see them, but if you're looking down at him (on a walk, for example) or behind him, what then?

Luckily, for many short-haired breeds at least, there's an easy answer to the problem. When eyes zoom in on their target and facial muscles react accordingly, the smooth area on top of his head between the ears becomes furrowed with deep wrinkles. (A similar thing happens to our foreheads when we raise our eyebrows.) It's much harder to see with longer-haired breeds, but is so obvious on dogs such as Rottweilers and Staffordshire bull terriers that it's visible from several feet away. With the right dog, it's a great early warning beacon of tension building, but also of more benign alertness. From the context, and with intimate prior knowledge of your dog, you'll know the difference instinctively.

In the case of a dog on the point of snapping, you may see the stiffness extend to the neck. Without moving his head, he's not looking face-on towards his target, but slightly sideways; not moving his head or body, but following with his eyes, creating the visible whites of the eyes effect I referred to earlier in the book. It's often the eerie calm before the storm. He's on edge – and you should be on your guard.

At the same time – and this varies a lot from dog to dog – you may see hackles rising on the back of his neck or along his spine. Hackles are an aspect of dogs that I think is often misunderstood. It might be a sign of impending doom – he's angry, to slightly over-humanise it – or alternatively, he may be excited in a completely different, better way. Hackles aren't necessarily bad news, but they could be, depending on the circumstances. I've seen dogs raise their hackles when greeting friends, for example, and in that case there's nothing to worry about. The hackles reflex is just that: an involuntary action that happens when an animal is aroused in one of many ways. It happens with the human animal, too. Have you ever felt the hair on the back of your neck stand up for some reason? Or on your forearms? Goosebumps when you're not cold? That's human hackles, and it happens for a whole spectrum of reasons. Now you know how it feels for your dog.

Incidentally, if you see a dog turning away from another dog or a person, but they look less tense and are *looking* away too, the chances are that they're averting their eyes in deference. It's a submissive, 'I am not challenging you' kind of thing. (Again, I'm humanising dogs a little too much here, on purpose. I've always found it helps people understand dogs if it's explained in this way.)

We've all seen dogs shaking water off their fur (as seen in slow motion video in 1,001 TV ads for laundry and floor cleaning products, almost always featuring improbably dirty dogs). Have you ever noticed a dog shaking off when she's not wet, though? There's a reason for it. When dogs are tense because something scary or anxiety-inducing happened, there's a need to unlock the tension in the muscles when it's over and they calm down again. Shaking-off is the perfect way. The human equivalent is when we exhale a big sigh and allow our bodies to relax. Shake-offs are a dog's way to say, 'Phew!'

Interesting, isn't it? I'm always attentive to shake-offs. They're usually quite predictable and I know that better behaviour will shortly follow, but sometimes they tell me about something I missed (I'm only human after all). There are times I see a shake-off and only then realise what preceded must have been more stressful for the dog than she was letting on. It's a silent communication that translates as, 'I'm glad that's over,' occasionally when we had no idea she was quite so nervous. If you fancy a spot of dog watching, next time you're at the vet's keep an eye on the dogs leaving. You'll see plenty of shake-offs.

Shake-offs happen frequently, possibly more so than you realised until now. Keep your eyes out for shake-offs and you'll start to see them everywhere. Every one provides useful information.

I promised I'd end this brief discussion about whole-body signals on a positive note, and here it is. Cue drum roll ... *Ladies and gentlemen, please welcome on stage the* ... fanfare ... *play bow*. If you're unfamiliar with the phrase, don't worry because, as a dog lover, you'll almost certainly have experienced it already. Puppies do it a lot and many adult dogs still play bow to initiate play with other dogs and with their people.

With their bottom high in the air, and often with their tails wagging, they plant their front on the floor, their legs pointed all the way forwards, towards the object of their affection, and then they stretch. And stretch. (If you know yoga, think downward-facing dog.) If you're the chosen one, you're honoured. Especially honoured if they do a double play bow: stretching the front legs and then the back legs by reversing the move. Little dogs often do a version of a play bow that involves putting both front paws on your leg and stretching up against you.

What does a play bow mean? Essentially, it's, 'You're nice. Let's play.' Some folks, who are given to flights of fancy, will have you believe it means, 'I love you'. Obviously, I cannot condone such blatant anthropomorphism. I am, however, given to flights of fantasy. And I love dogs.

So, as they say in the old cartoons, 'That's all, folks.' I've covered as much as I can here about how to read your dog. I've restricted myself to the most important points, or where I thought there were myths to bust, or something interesting to add that most dog owners may not know. I sincerely hope you've learned interesting things so far.

If you'd like to know more about how to read your dog than I've given here, good for you – I encourage you to read around the subject. There are a number of good books and websites that cover the subject of dog body language, and scientific studies are being undertaken all the time. Read as much as you can, but don't believe everything you read (especially on the internet).

We're also at the end of part one. If you've read through all of my principles, give yourself a pat on the back. You're now equipped with a distillation of the knowledge it's taken me over a decade, working with thousands of dogs (not to mention owners), to glean. Theory is great, but it's only a start. Practice (and a few mistakes along the way) puts it all into context.

In part two, we'll have a look at how it comes together in the real world. Step this way . . .

Part Two

Chapter 14

Getting a puppy (or the mysterious case of the missing stair)

Having two large-breed puppies has a detrimental effect on your ability to keep everything shipshape and Bristol-fashion. Not only do you have less time to devote to the dubious pleasures of housework, but they go about their business – eat-play-toilet-sleep-repeat – in a way that undoes all your good work. Hey presto, a double whammy.

In all honesty, my house in the early 2000s wasn't the tidiest before Axel arrived, but it went downhill steadily for nine months until Gordon joined him. Then it completely fell off a cliff.

It came to a head one day when I came back from the shops to find the bottom stair all-but missing and two black-and-tan teddy bears looking very pleased with themselves. Clearly, the carpet had been an agreeable tuggy-toy (but not for long), and the wood tasted delicious.

'Have you quite finished, Axel?' I imagined myself saying. (I have a lot of fantasy conversations with dogs.)

'I'm absolutely stuffed,' he'd reply, in the manner of *Monty Python*'s Mr Creosote. 'I couldn't eat another thing.'

Puppies are lovely but make no mistake, they are hard work and having two at the same time is double the trouble. It's entirely doable, but you will need eyes in the back of your head.

Getting a puppy should begin with choosing a reputable breeder or rescue centre. If you're looking for a pedigree dog in the UK, you could do worse than visit the Kennel Club website for information and breeder listings. For crossbreeds – no bad thing as they are often healthier – asking around in online forums and seeking personal recommendations from dog owners you trust is often the best option. It's probably wise not to take everything you hear at face value, but it will provide a decent overview.

In any case, it's important to avoid puppy farms, where the main driver is money, and not breeding puppies with good health and temperament prospects. Always ask to see the puppy's mother and the place where the puppies are being brought up. Inside the breeder's house is ideal. Ask if it's possible to return the puppy if things don't work out. Of course, it's the last thing anyone wants, but good breeders will always say yes and may insist on first refusal. Be suspicious if you're offered a choice of several different breeds, because most good breeders focus on one or two. Finally, don't be fobbed off by a breeder insisting you pick up a puppy from a neutral location, such as a service station. They may be trying to hide the conditions your puppy came from. On the other hand – and this applies to rehoming organisations, too – if you feel as though *you* are the one being grilled as to *your* suitability, that's good – they clearly care about the home the dog is going to.

For as long as I can remember, the accepted norm has been for puppies to move to their new homes when they're around eight weeks old. I heard recently that UK Guide Dogs release puppies from their mother at seven weeks to start the long process of socialisation and training. It got me thinking, because there's no doubt they know how best to train and care for assistance dogs. It made me reassess what we've always been told: that eight weeks is the ideal time for a puppy to move on. Had I (and most dog behaviour experts) got that wrong?

It turns out that much of what we know about dogs' early development is more than half a century old. It comes from *Genetics and the Social Behavior of the Dog* by J.P. Scott and J.L. Fuller, published in 1965, which summarises 13 years of scientific study at the Jackson Laboratories in Bar Harbor, Maine, in the United States. According to the research, the socialisation period starts at week three and lasts until week 14. During this time, puppies interact with their littermates and mother, practising playing and hunting and – provided they have plenty of positive exposure with humans and our environment (homes, cars, traffic, other pets, you name it) – they also bond with people and become well-rounded pets.

The suggestion is that socialisation with other dogs happens first (from around three to six weeks) and with people and the environment next (from six weeks, until the final curtain comes down on socialisation at 14 weeks). Dogs that missed out on socialisation as puppies turn up all too regularly in my behavioural consultations.

Next, I looked at more recent research on socialisation and found an article in the journal *Veterinary Record* with the catchy title of 'Prevalence of owner-reported behaviours in dogs separated from the litter at two different ages', reporting a study from the University of Milan which involved 140 dogs over a period of many years. Half the dogs had been removed from the litter when they were 30–40 days old (approximately four to five weeks); the other half at 60 days (between eight and nine weeks).

The owners of all 140 dogs filled in detailed questionnaires when their dogs were between 18 months and seven years of age, reporting on the dogs' adult behaviour. The summary of the results is an eye-opener: '*The odds of displaying destructiveness, excessive barking, fearfulness on walks, reactivity to noises, toy possessiveness, food possessiveness and attention-seeking were significantly greater for the dogs that had been removed from the litter earlier during the socialisation period.*'

Interesting, isn't it? So, take pet puppies away from their mothers too early (earlier than guide dogs) and you'll likely impact their chances of being happy, well-adjusted dogs in later life; leave it too late and you'll miss the socialisation period altogether. How late is too late? Well, if we take 14 weeks to be the endpoint it means you'll have needed to get lots of good interactions in before that particular line in the sand.

So, when's the ideal time for your puppy to leave its mother? Seven weeks if you're recruiting for Guide Dogs UK. They know their breeding inside out and have a specialised socialisation and training programme that's been fine-tuned over decades and with thousands of dogs. It's followed by expert foster carers and trainers and the end results are smart and happy assistance dogs.

For the rest of us mere mortals, having reviewed all the evidence, I've come to a very unsatisfactory conclusion. Much as there's little in life I love more than debunking an old dog behaviour myth, the fact of the matter is the conventional wisdom holds true: eight weeks is about right. Leave it later, and you're giving your puppy less time to socialise before the 14-week cut-off. Any earlier and you'll need collective knowledge, skill and dedication at the level of Guide Dogs UK to pull it off. That's a bet you probably shouldn't make.

Socialisation is more than simply being sociable with other dogs and puppies. It's about communicating appropriately with people and other pets, too – but even that is only half the story. There's a whole learning process to cover that prepares puppies to be confident and happy in all the environments they will encounter in life. The aim is to create hundreds, if not thousands, of little positive experiences that engage all the puppy's senses, including new sights, sounds, smells, textures and even tastes.

What we're aiming for is your puppy to log many hours of good experiences, so that she's well prepared for anything that life might throw at her. Pilots logging flying hours spring to mind. The more hours logged – in the widest of circumstances – the better. Ideally without crashing.

Your demeanour is absolutely key throughout the process. If your puppy is looking to you to judge how to react to, for example, a man in fluorescent jacket, the best way to convince her is to adopt a business-as-usual demeanour and tone. She's thinking, 'This is a weird animal,' but your manner needs to suggest that, 'It's fine, and I'm not worried by him.'

If she does have an adverse reaction to something – looking fearful or barking, for example – make a mental note and carry on with what you were doing. Whatever you do, don't force her to experience more of it right now in the hope you'll fix it, because you'll likely make it worse. Don't look anxious either or she'll pick up on it (and you might be surprised how easy it is for anxious body language to leak out if you're concerned things are going wrong).

Resolve to practise the scary thing another day, possibly from a greater distance (or on a lower volume if it's a sound). The motto here is: keep calm and carry on. Expect good and bad days and don't let the bad ones throw you off course. Progress is rarely linear.

To cover more sounds than would normally be possible, try an internet search for downloadable soundtracks designed for dog socialisation. Play them around the house when you're around (never when you're out). Start on low volume, increasing slowly over a period of weeks. Pay no attention to them and the message you're putting across will be clear: the world is full of unusual noises and that's OK.

Most of us wear shoes when we pop to the shops. Not so dogs. We're isolated from the textures underfoot in a way our canine friends aren't, so make sure you give your puppy the opportunity to feel different surfaces as soon as your vet advises it is safe for them to walk around outdoors. Indoors, shiny floors seem to cause the most problems for dogs in later life, so – especially if your place is carpeted throughout – have a think about friends' houses or public spaces you can visit to provide a variety of experiences. The more the merrier.

On the subject of friends, invite them to yours in ones, twos and then finally small groups. Visitors of all kinds are normal for most of us so, whether it's friends, tradespeople or parcel deliveries, show your dog they're all welcome.

Although it's not normally included in socialisation discussions, I think giving puppies the opportunity to experience as many good-quality puppy foods as possible makes sense. I've always fed a selection and never raised a picky dog yet. To put it another way, if you exclusively feed Super-Dooper Chicken for breakfast, lunch and dinner for six months, you probably shouldn't be too surprised when you serve up Fabulously Non-Farty Duck à l'Orange flavour for the first time and she looks down her snout at you as if to say, 'Luvvie ... darling ... I couldn't possibly!'

There are plenty of online socialisation checklists to use as a starting point. They're very helpful and you should use them as inspiration to draw up your own list, making sure you cover everything that will apply in your world. Take sewing machines, for example. I don't think my Rottweilers ever saw one. I've never seen them on socialisation checklists either, but if sewing's your thing, make sure it's on your list. They are, after all, scary clackety-clack biting monsters that eat cloth and fingers. Unless, that is, you know otherwise. Motorbike? Monster. Football on the telly? Sharpen your pencil and get writing. You'll be surprised how many monsters lurk in your life.

It's important to cover everything on your list on many occasions, but not always in the same location. Puppies struggle to generalise, that is to take something they learned in certain surroundings and apply it to others. For example, take a bin lorry on the high street. A puppy doesn't automatically take the learning (bin lorries *generally* make a heck of a row, but aren't out to get us) and transfer it, for example, to a bin lorry outside your house. To understand bin lorries are safe everywhere, puppies need to experience them repeatedly in different places.

Socialisation takes significant time and effort for a few weeks. It is, however, hugely rewarding to see the progress and know your hard work is creating a bulletproof dog for many years to come. You only have one chance to get it right. Make the best of it.

Chapter 15

Dogs aren't teenagers. Oh, hang on . . .

'Don't forget . . .' Axel's breeder's words were ringing in my ears as we very gingerly drove off with him on a cold, bright February morning in 2006, 'he'll get to six months and act as though he's completely forgotten every bit of training you've ever taught him. Don't panic. He'll come out the other side before he's one and he'll be fine.'

It was the first time I'd heard about dogs having a teenage phase, but she was absolutely right. Winter turned to spring and, by early summer, Axel turned teenage. I had previously been rather proud of his 'sit' and 'down'; I'd say the command once only and he'd be there like a shot, every time. Not any more. I'd repeat myself or try different tones of voice, all to little effect. He'd grunt like a human teenager roused from a deep slumber before midday and then ignore me.

It was utterly hopeless. All I could do was hunker down and wait for the adult Axel to emerge, like a 50kg black-and-tan butterfly, from his furry chrysalis. Except by then Gordon had arrived, bang on schedule to start his own anarchic adolescence at about the time one-year-old Axel would – hopefully – be growing out of his. Oh, the joys of puppy parenthood!

They turned out well, it has to be said, and we had a lovely decade of companionship ahead of us but, boy, were the adolescent months hard. Since then, I've come across the teenage dog phenomenon so many times I've lost count. I've told my clients that it's definitely a thing, even if the science wasn't entirely there to prove it. Hold your nerve when it hits, I'll say, keep doing the right things and you'll weather the storm.

The physiological changes dogs undergo have been understood for a long time. Most female dogs have their first season between six and 12 months of age and, at the same time, the majority of male dogs feel the effects of something new and powerful: testosterone.

The behavioural knock-on effect hadn't been studied until 2020, when the University of Newcastle analysed data from about 285 dogs; a combination of behavioural tests and questionnaires filled in by the dogs' caregivers. When the results were in, a clear picture emerged: there was indeed a significant worsening of dog obedience in the middle of the teenage period (around eight months of age) compared to their previously good puppy behaviour at five months. Teenage dogs were found to be more than twice as likely to require multiple commands before responding. On a brighter note, behaviour markedly improved after the adolescent phase, at around 12 months.

Similarities with teenage humans abound. Researchers also noted that adolescent dogs appear to reserve their most disobedient behaviour for primary caregivers, behaving better with strangers or other less familiar people, such as a dog trainer. I remember my glowing school reports being read with incredulity by my mum and dad because, by all accounts, the model pupil act didn't extend far beyond the school gates.

Here's how the scientists summarised their findings: '*In most dogs, it seems that adolescent-phase disobedient behaviour exists, but does not last. Unfortunately, the welfare consequences . . . could be lasting because this corresponds with the peak age at which dogs are relinquished to shelters.*'*

Isn't that interesting? It's a good job we don't have rescue centres for human teenagers, eh? Then again . . .

---

* https://royalsocietypublishing.org/doi/10.1098/rsbl.2020.0097

Chapter 16

Lovely but loony: adventures with a rehomed dog

My current dog, Lily, came along as a rehome dog a couple of years ago. I've long been of the opinion that there's no right and wrong when it comes to choosing between getting a puppy or taking on an adult dog that's being rehomed: a lot depends on personal circumstances. I've brought up puppies before, but this time – since I don't have the lifestyle or time these days to devote to a puppy in their first few months – I went looking for an adult dog instead.

Lily, a three-year-old Labrador/boxer-cross, bounced into my life soon after. She's an unusual mix and not something I was especially looking for, but all the better for it. Being all black, she looks very Labrador, but her behaviour is more bouncy boxer – at least until there's any food around and then she's torn two ways at once by her genetics: Ball! Cheese! Ball! Cheese! Ball! Cheese . . . ! Cheese always wins.

She's delightful in most every way. Clever, too. But there is a little thing I hadn't spotted until she was home. A boxer thing. She loves climbing fences. First it was the four-foot post-and-rail job that separated my back garden from the farmer's field – and sheep – behind. One day I turned my back on her for all of three seconds and when I looked back she was mooching about on the other side, looking very pleased with herself and calmly sniffing about for sheep poo (delicious, apparently). I got her back *tout suite* and resolved to raise the fence by a couple of feet.

An hour later and the job was done. I was admiring my handiwork from the field side, unable to get back into the garden without walking around the houses, when Lily, not to be outdone, rocketed up the six-foot fence separating our garden from the neighbours' garden, scrabbling over it like a monster squirrel and playing catch-me-if-you-can with their cocker spaniel. He couldn't and nor could the neighbours. She whirled like a furry dervish through the French doors and around the dining room, playing skittles with furniture. This Keystone Cops farce might have gone on much longer had she not felt the call of nature and returned to the perfectly manicured lawn as I looked on, helpless and horrified, while she deposited a steaming pile of poo so enormous it could probably be seen from space.

'Sorry about that,' I said, breaking a stupefied silence of several seconds. 'This is Lily, by the way.' It was one hell of an introduction. 'I'll get a poo bag.'

If you're looking for a rehome dog, you could do a lot worse than to start with the big national organisations, but many established local rescues do a great job, too. Ask around your local dog-owning community. If you have a breed in mind, the Kennel Club's website-based Find a Rescue service has a very comprehensive list of UK breed-specific organisations.

Have a long think about your lifestyle and energy levels and be honest with the rehoming organisation about your environment and experience level so they can help you choose. Temperament – both yours and the dog's – is more important than looks if you want a perfect pet partner. Some breeds need a lot of exercise, for example, and can go stir crazy if they don't get enough. Border collies spring to mind – perfect for an avid fell runner but less so for many of us. But bear in mind, too, that all dogs are individuals. I've met laid-back collies and, more rarely, reactive Labradors, so take each dog on their own merits. Size comes into it, of course, as does the depth of your pockets (bigger dogs eat more – no surprise there – but veterinary treatment and insurance is often more costly, too). For me, though, temperament is the biggest deal.

Be aware that rescue organisations are usually run by the loveliest people who want the best for the dogs, which means that occasionally they might understate issues just a little, so as not to put you off a dog. They mean well, and I'm sure they don't want to say anything bad about the dog, but it can lead to problems further down the line.

I'm certainly not saying you shouldn't take on a dog with issues. No dog (or owner, come to that) is perfect, but you should know about any in advance and be prepared to call in a little professional help if necessary. Just be honest with yourself and what you can cope with.

It takes time to bond with your rescue dog when you get them home. They've been through a lot, even if they haven't been mistreated in any way, and trust takes weeks or months to build up. I'd be especially careful not to let them off-lead anywhere insecure until you're sure they'll come back. There's a strong instinct for a dog to explore the new environment, including where their old home lies in relation to the new, unfamiliar place. In Lily's case that would have involved a long trip down the M40, but I wouldn't have put it past her in those first few days.

Dog people are sometimes given to flights of emotional fancy. We can't help ourselves (and yes, I'm including myself here because, much as it's my job to rise above the fog of emotion to see clearly, I'm a dog lover at heart). You'll hear people say rescue dogs are forever grateful to their loving owners. It's not very scientific – I don't even know how you'd set about proving that scientifically. But when your new dog comes to you dangling a poorly paw in the air with a look that says, 'You're my person, please help,' or snuggles up on the sofa and contentedly falls asleep on you for the first time, then you'll know: she's found her home. And it's not bricks and mortar. It's you.

Chapter 17
Kids and dogs

Preparing for a baby is a big deal at the best of times, and more so if there's a dog in the household. Planning should ideally begin as soon as you discover you're pregnant, but it's more typical for clients to call me a couple of weeks before the due date, asking for a transformed dog. There's a lot we can do in a short time, but the stakes are high.

I was once honoured to be at a client's house doing a consultation on the day the baby came home from Northampton General Hospital. We'd planned the date in advance, but the baby decided she wanted to be in on the act too, so entered the world two weeks early. It all ended with a happy family (and a previously growly Labrador who doted on his little sister), but talk about pressure . . .

Much worse, though, was the case of an infant who was ten months old and crawling when she was bitten in the face by the family dog. I'm no stranger to people doing silly and regrettable things with their dogs, but this case really shocked me because of the lack of awareness from parents who should have known better.

The dog had a six-year history of biting people when

challenged. You might reasonably have thought when they found out they were having a baby that they'd try to seek help, but no. Nor did they when the baby was born. They waited until after the child was crawling. The inevitable happened one day when it is thought (there were no adults in the room at the time) the crawling infant inadvertently cornered the dog in the sitting room.

I suspended judgement and reminded myself that the mother, who had been in the kitchen, was probably full of remorse and didn't need a lecture. But there was something that had to be said.

'Look, I'm going to say something that I'm sure you already know,' I said, doing my best to be tactful, 'but you should never leave a child and a dog unsupervised. Any dog.'

'Do you think so?' she replied.

What? My mind was doing somersaults. Yes, I did think so!

'He's a pet dog,' she continued. 'Can't you train him so we can leave them long enough for me to make a cup of tea?'

What exactly do you say to a woman who thinks like that when you know she's on maternity leave from her local authority child protection job? I was speechless.

Thankfully, it is very rare that people think like this, so let's focus on getting it right in the first place and consider the actions to take before and after the birth. It's important to note that the advice that follows assumes a reasonably well-behaved family pet with no pre-existing aggression issues. If you have a dog whose behaviour you were already worried about before you became pregnant, please seek professional help.

It is entirely possible your dog knew you were pregnant

before you did since their sensitive noses pick up on the tiniest of hormonal changes. So it makes sense to make a few changes before the baby arrives. The aim should be to avoid your dog associating the new arrival with bad things, such as the inevitable loss of centre-of-attention status.

Start by giving your dog a little less attention than before and by creating a little 'me time' for yourself. Teach him that you like him being calmly by himself in his bed or crate by praising him when he settles down. If he's clamouring for attention, you might as well start now to ignore his pestering because, when you're in mid-nappy change later, there will be no choice.

If there need to be physical changes in the layout of your house – such as moving where your dog is fed or where he sleeps – now's the time to make them. If you allow your dog on the sofa currently, you might want to think about changing that. I'm not a stickler for no dogs on sofas ordinarily, but it's going to be a handy sanctuary for you and your baby when the time comes. Make it out of bounds now and things will be so much smoother later.

Similarly, you'll want to keep the dog's toys separate from the baby's. You'll no doubt be given a few baby items nearer to the time, but it's a good idea to get a few now and to teach him that he's a good boy for playing with his own but that baby's things aren't his to chew.

Until now, when something that looked and smelled like a child's toy appeared in the house, it was invariably for him. The easiest way to teach this is to hold a baby toy and, when he approaches to investigate, firmly tell him 'no', using your best head teacher face. You can use your other hand to move him away if necessary. When he starts backing off voluntarily, praise him and give him a toy of his own to play with.

The final thing you might want to do before your baby arrives is to change a few routines. Just as you'll be giving your dog less attention, you'll have less time to walk him too, or perhaps you'll do it at different times. If you're thinking of getting a little help from a dog walker or a friend, then start at least a week or two before your due date. Make all these preparations before the baby arrives, and you'll smooth the way for everyone, including your dog.

As much as you prepare, suddenly there's a baby in the family and you'll be faced with introducing your dog to the new family member. If there's an opportunity to bring something that smells of mum and baby back from hospital, that's great, but think carefully about how you might want your dog to interact with it. Don't do as one new dad I met did, and hand over a baby blanket to an excited Jack Russell only to see him rag it around and then take it apart with his teeth, yarn by yarn. It's not exactly the association we're after.

Instead, keep hold of the item and let him sniff it gently when he's tired and cuddled up with you. Discourage him from getting excited. The clear message here is, 'When you smell this scent, be a good boy. Be calm.'

Before introducing your dog to the baby, take him for a long walk. Let him have a run to blow off a little energy if you like, but make sure the last part of the walk home is steady and plodding. We want a calm – not hyped-up – dog. If you can, time it so the baby is asleep when you get back. We don't want your dog's first encounter to be stressful.

Decide in advance to split the parenting roles for the next

few minutes between dog and baby duties. Bring your dog into the room (there's no reason you can't keep him on-lead if you want, but don't allow tension in the lead). It's useful if the baby isn't on the floor, but asleep in a cot at roughly doggy eye level.

Approach, but keep a couple of feet away and praise him if he's curious, as he's bound to be, but calm. If he gets over-excited, take him out and try again in a couple of minutes. If he's getting pushy, use your hand between him and the baby to create a block. We're looking for him to keep a respectful distance of a couple of feet initially and for him to stay calm. If he does, don't hold back showing him you love him for it. But don't rev him up, either. Keep repeating these short and sweet meetings and he'll soon understand.

Dogs instinctively know what families and new babies are about. There's a massive difference between domestic dogs and wolves, of course, but some things don't change. Encoded deep in the DNA is the knowledge that we all live in social groups and sometimes little ones appear. Mother Nature has prepared your dog better than you or I ever could.

Chapter 18

Puppy recall and the curious tale of the baby Rottweiler

When Axel was about 12 weeks old, I took him to a field near where I lived to let him off-lead in the big wide world for the first time. We'd been doing plenty of puppy recall in the back garden and it had been going very well; I was reassured that puppies follow those they've bonded with like little ducklings.

At least, every puppy I'd encountered at that time did. I unclipped the lead, walked away and called him with a bright and happy voice as I'd done so many times in the garden. Nothing. He looked at me, turned on his heel and started waddling away. I called again. He stopped in his tracks, looked at me for a second or two, and turned again to go.

I had a trick up my sleeve, though. A sure-fire, deploy-only-in-the-case-of-puppy-emergency tactic that would have him coming back like a good 'un. I called again, he paused and looked at me and, before he had chance to look back again, I turned on my heel and walked away from him. That would show him. Certain that he'd panic and realise he didn't want to be lost, he'd run to me as quickly as his little legs could carry him. I walked on. 'Hold your nerve,' I told myself. 'You'll hear the patter of tiny paws any moment.'

I didn't. This was a battle of wills. Man versus baby Rottweiler. An intrusive thought occurred to me. When I'd last seen him, he was walking towards the main road. He was a fair distance from it, but he was heading into danger. I couldn't bear the thought. I turned around, still hoping to see him running to me, but no: there he was, nonchalantly toddling off, not a care in the world.

The message was clear. I don't need you. Thanks for the free food and all that, but I'm off to make my own way in life now, find a girlfriend and settle down. See ya! I caved in, ran the length of the field and picked him up. Final score: Axel one, Dad nil.

Axel was one of a kind. It's unlikely you'll ever encounter such a headstrong puppy. Certainly, I haven't in the 13 years and thousands of dog and puppy consultations since. For the other 99 per cent of puppies, then, the following notes apply.

I can't stress enough the importance of puppy training. That you only get one chance to give them the best start in life sounds like a corny line from a puppy-class leaflet (there's a reason for that), but it's true. Puppies are pre-programmed to learn from the people they trust.

The best way to train recall is to start young and build up a great habit before they hit the rebellious teenage stage. Let's use our puppy's eagerness for fun and food to our advantage, shall we?

I've had a lot of puppies through my hands in the years

since Axel was little. Here's how I used to do it with puppies in classes.

First, choose a food treat that your puppy would have your hand off for. It should be super-tasty, but just a morsel. We don't want to fill her up and we do want her, literally, coming back for more.

Place yourself just a metre away from her, no further. Many dog owners make the mistake of starting much too far away – we're teaching, not testing. Show your puppy what you have in your hand and, when she moves towards you, scoot backwards so she has to speed up to catch you. You don't need to move far – perhaps a metre or two – but enough to create a game that draws upon her hunting instinct and her love of tasty food.

In effect, we're saying 'catch me if you can' and making sure she does, every time. Don't ever be tempted to take the food to her if she doesn't come to you. That's a sure way of rewarding the wrong behaviour. Put the food away and try again later.

We will need a recall command, a shorthand label for 'run to me like a little rocket'. I'd suggest 'come' or 'come here', but any distinct sounds will do. Incidentally, if you're ever likely to use 'heel' as a walking instruction, you might want to avoid 'here' for recall. The two words are confusingly similar. Pick something that comes naturally and stick to it.

As she's running to you, be excited with your command and encouragement. Let it ring out in a bright and happy tone. You may have noticed I used this phrase earlier; I've done it on purpose. Bright and happy is my go-to description of the sound I'm after. If you only remember one thing from this chapter, please make it this. In almost everything other than recall I'm a big fan of calm praise for pet dog training, but there's a time and a place. No one wants a calm, plodding recall and so this is the time to go bonkers. Speed, excitement and fun are where it's at.

Note that at this stage you'll be calling the command as she runs, not before, to make the association with running back quickly as it is happening. Once you have your puppy coming back, start extending the distance between you. Always train in short bursts of a few recalls a session because we want her to be keen for next time, not bored with it all.

Finally, try your recall command when she's not expecting it, but not from very far away. This is the moment of truth. Does she really know what it means? Will she come without you creating the chase-me game first? If you've practised enough, she will. Start extending the distance again and throw in the odd recall when you're just out of sight.

Using your puppy's name with a recall command is fine, but it's not a substitute. The name should get attention and the recall instruction tells her what to do: they serve different functions. I put a short pause of no more than a second between the two. Here's how your puppy translates it. 'Lily!' (Ooh, that's me!) – *pause* – 'Come!' ('Yay, run!')

You can't start this training too early and I'd absolutely do it before your puppy is old enough to run free outdoors. There should be no negative consequences in puppy recall if she doesn't come back. If she rockets back to you, great. If not, there's no telling off, but no fun or treat to be had either. She'll figure it out quickly enough.

Gone with the wind – when recall goes wrong

I was out walking the other evening along a bridleway which roller-coasters its way across the hills near where I live. I was in my own world, listening to an audio book on earphones, when a voice pierced the calm.

'Scarlett! Scaaar-lett!'

The moment was slightly surreal because there was no woman to be seen. I pulled out my earphones.

'Scarlett!' There it was again. I wasn't imagining it.

There was a woman somewhere the other side of the next crest, clearly distressed, looking for a dog. Or a daughter, perhaps.

'Scarlett, come!'

A dog, then. I walked on and she started to appear, first her head—

'Scarlett!'

Then her waxed-cotton torso—

'Scaaar-lett!'

Finally, the rest of her, dog lead in hand but no dog to show for it.

'Have you lost a dog?' I asked. It seemed like a silly question since Scarlett had quite clearly gone with the wind.

'Yes, have you seen her? She's a fox red Labrador.'

'No, I'm sorry, she hasn't come past me.'

The woman moved her frantic focus from the distant horizon and looked at me properly for the first time. A familiar spark of recognition lit up her face.

'Don't I know you?' she asked. (She didn't.) 'Oh! You're the dog man off the telly. How do I get her back?'

It was a perfectly reasonable question in the circumstances, but impossible to answer. This was like Lewis Hamilton happening across the scene of a road accident and a driver – who's simultaneously run out of road and skill – pointing at a crumpled car and asking, 'How do I uncrash this?'

I'd clean forgotten to pack my dog trainer's magic wand in my rucksack (remiss, I know), but of course I really wanted to help. What dog lover wouldn't?

'OK, well, she's not come my way, so she's either in the fields around us or somewhere behind you,' I said. 'How long has she been gone?'

'Twenty minutes, maybe.' The woman's eyes had reverted to scanning the distant hills. She looked utterly horror-struck as she started calling again.

I remembered when I, too, had been the owner of a lost dog – Gordon – over a decade ago. I'd not done enough recall training and chanced my arm one day. Big mistake. He ran off and it had been dark at the time, too. I called and called until I was hoarse, but it was useless. It's an awful feeling to lose a dog, not knowing if you'll see him again, where he'll be, out in the cold, if he'll survive. I struck lucky with Gordon. I discovered by chance something that no dog training book ever tells you.

'You should stop calling her now,' I said.

'What?!' The woman looked at me aghast. She wasn't about to give up the fight for Scarlett.

'Doing nothing right now is our best chance to get her back,' I said. 'I guess you've called a hundred times in the last

20 minutes. It was worth a try, but she's either in earshot or she isn't. As simple as that. If she can't hear us, there's no point calling. If she can, then frankly my dear, she doesn't give a damn. She knows exactly where you are and she knows she can stay out playing. Let's sit down and be quiet.'

It's counter-intuitive. Every fibre of your being wants to shout out for your lost dog, but by being quiet – as I found out by accident with Gordon – sometimes they wonder where you are and come running to find you. It's what happened with Scarlett, to everyone's relief (except perhaps the errant dog).

We were lucky with Scarlett because, although being quiet when you've lost a dog is a tool to keep at the bottom of the box just in case, let's be clear: it's car-crash dog training. Prevention, as they say, is always better than cure and the alternative is practise, practise, practise. If there's a short cut, I'm still to find it. When it comes to recall, there's simply no substitute for putting in the time and effort.

If you followed the steps outlined for puppy recall, you'll have a super-reliable dog when they're older. That's not to say you'll avoid all bumps along the way. Puppies turn into teenagers and some find 1,001 ingenious ways to be disobedient. Of course, we don't all get our dogs as puppies. When I rehomed Lily she was three years old and I taught her recall almost from scratch.

Whatever the age of your dog, all the puppy recall points serve as a good foundation. If your voice is flat or menacing or there's nothing worth coming back for, such as a treat (even if it's a variable-reward jackpot), then not coming back is likely to become a regular feature of your walks, sadly.

Recall is a great time to be practising a variable-reward system. If food is your reward of choice for recall, I'd advise something really special, like small pieces of chicken or ham. The operative word here is small, for a couple of reasons. Firstly, we're looking for the food equivalent of a tease: a hint of something tasty increasing the desire for more, and not lessening the attraction because she's getting full.

Secondly, we don't want to be encouraging our dog to run on a full stomach due to the risk of a potentially fatal twisted gut. For both reasons, I'd always choose to do recall training when my dog is hungry. Incidentally, if you've never heard of twisted gut, also known as gastric torsion, take a minute or two for an internet search. Medical conditions are beyond the scope of this book, but it's something all dog owners should know about.

Once you've established what your dog's favourite treat is, reserve it for recall training and don't let them have it at other times. We want to make coming back to you not just attractive, but really special. 'Run back and get chicken? Dead right!' rather than, 'Not chicken again! Meh.'

As with puppies, once they've locked onto you and your treat, you'll want to run backwards, still facing your dog if you can (and it's safe to do so). Have a quick glance behind you for divots, small children, abandoned mine shafts, unexploded bombs, that kind of thing. Dogs love to chase and, by triggering that impulse, especially with adult dogs, you're laying down a challenge. Want what I've got? Catch me if you can – if you think you're fast enough. They do, and they are, so use it to your advantage.

Train in an area without distractions first. You'll want to

get the basics imprinted before making it more difficult for your dog to comply. Choose a place or a time when it's going to be quiet and avoid dog walkers, cyclists or squirrels that may derail your plans.

Only once you have achieved a rock-solid recall can you move things up a notch. Think of it this way: if your dog's not coming back 100 per cent when it's quiet, how on earth will he cope if it's busy? We don't want to set him up to fail by trying too hard, too soon. Build up distractions slowly but surely.

If you choose to use a long lead with a dog that's inclined to run off, I'd suggest getting a purpose-made dog recall lead of about ten metres, one similar to, but much lighter than, a lunge rein for a horse. I much prefer a simple long line to a retractable lead. The problem with retractables for recall training is that there's always a little spring-loaded tension at the dog's end. If you train with tension, when the day finally comes to unleash him – the moment of truth – you'll likely find Fido shoots off into the distance because his new-found freedom feels so different.

With an ordinary line, you're in control of the tension, but if it's allowed to become taut you'll have the same problem. Conversely, if you allow it to trail along the ground your dog will get himself all tangled up. It's a fact that a dog can only get tangled up in a line if he steps over it before the person the other end takes up the slack. Keeping it off the ground – but not tight – is quite a skill with a moving dog, but it comes with practice.

Practice. There I go again. If there's one word that sums up recall training . . .

Chapter 19

Lead walking – the dog who thought he was a Land Rover

'Hang on a sec, Graeme, he needs to pee.' I was out walking the other day in a park near Castleford in Yorkshire with a client and his collie/poodle-cross. We ground to a halt while Eric (the dog, not the man) did his thing and then let us walk on ten paces before we were forced to stop again.

'Sorry, mate, he does this a lot,' said Eric's owner, embarrassed but resigned.

'How many times does he stop you on a walk?' I asked.

'Oh, about every two or three minutes. But I've always been told that it's his walk and it's important to let them sniff and explore.'

'OK,' I said, 'let's break that down. If you go out for an hour and he stops you, say, every three minutes, that's 20 times. And you comply every time?'

'Pretty much. I know what you're going to say . . . He's in charge, isn't he?'

'Ha ha, yes, he is. Think of it as him saying, "Oi, you! Stop!" and you dutifully obey, 20 times. When he's done, he's telling you to walk on. That's "You may proceed" in dog speak. I bet you wouldn't stand for that from a child, but you do from your dog. That's another 20 commands of course, so 40 altogether in an hour's walk. I think you might be right – he is in charge!'

Eric, despite being half-poodle, had been named after a Viking, and yet a more un-Vikinglike dog you could not imagine. He was scared of his own shadow and was always highly strung on walks, a sort of confused and frightened half-French Viking with a Yorkshire accent. More Alan Bennett than Geoffrey Boycott.

Because he was constantly on edge, when other dogs came up to Eric he'd bark and snap to get rid of them. That usually worked, of course, but in any case he didn't have other options.

The man he was tethered to, like a whacking great human land anchor, prevented any chance of running away and he clearly wasn't in charge. If he wouldn't step up, then Eric would have to, the only way he knew how: fight. Or pretend to.

'The thing is, Jim,' I said, 'stopping to let him sniff on his terms seems unconnected to the problem he has with other dogs, but it's not. In order not to react out of fear, he has to be able to trust you enough to hand over responsibility for his safety. Instead, 40 times a walk you're saying, "Yes, sir, sorry, sir, can we go now please, sir?" What's a dog to think? When he barks at a dog and you tell him to pack it in, he's looking at you thinking, "Who the hell do you think YOU are? I'm in charge (even though I haven't the faintest clue what I'm doing). Stand back! I'll deal with this."'

In fairness to Jim, it's something I've seen from Cowdenbeath to Colchester. Castleford was no exception. It is true that dogs need to sniff around and explore, even to mark territory to some extent. The point that's usually missed is that this doesn't have to be on their terms. For people, there's a time to work and a time to play. There's no reason it can't be that way for dogs, too.

The problem starts with our mindset. 'I'm just popping out to walk the dog,' we say. Wrong. You're not walking the dog. You're going for a nice walk around the neighbourhood and you've decided to take your little loyal friend, Fido, with you, out of the goodness of your heart. OK, you and I know you are doing it for his sake as much as yours, but let's not tell him that. You should set the agenda, starting with the way you leave the house.

'Always go through a door first,' has been the advice given by dog experts since time immemorial. The logic is that leaders go first, others follow. It seems to make sense, except it's not always the case, even in the animal kingdom. There are times when you will want to send your dog through a door or threshold ahead of you. It's not necessarily the one who goes first who's the leader; it's the one who *decides*. If I give my dog the signal to jump in the back of the car, I don't jump in the boot myself first. She's not allowed to jump until I ask her either (if she does jump in without being asked I'll take a few moments to bring her back out and go through it again). Ultimately, though, I let her get in the car before me.

So it is with doors. If it's convenient to let Fido outside

while you sort out locking the door, that's fine so long as it's your decision, not his. Let him choose to drag you outside and you're already starting the walk on the wrong foot; instead, take a few moments until he's calmed down (you can get him to sit if you want) and then either walk through the door first, send him through, or let him come with you. Either way, you've started as you mean to go on – in control. Even if it takes five minutes, I'd consider it time well spent.

I split my own dog walks into periods I think of as 'on duty' and 'break time'. We're either in one mode or the other. I start with my dog walking nicely alongside. I decide when to stop, where to go and at what speed. That's 'on duty'. She has a job to do, but it's a really easy one – play follow-my-leader and do what I do.

Break time is, as it sounds, when Lily gets to sniff around, go to the toilet and, within reason, do whatever she wants. If I'm somewhere she shouldn't be off-lead (a motorway service station, for example), I'll let the lead run to its full length to give her a little more freedom. At other times, when it's safe, she'll be off-lead. When she's on a break, I'll happily follow where she wants to go if it suits me. It's her time, but I choose when it happens. I also choose the number of breaks on a walk because there's no reason we cannot alternate between 'on duty' and 'break' several times an hour.

Let's not forget that walking a dog is meant to be pleasurable for all concerned. I'm not suggesting that 'on duty' is regimented to the extent it's a military route march, some gruelling yomp across the enemy terrain that is the neighbouring housing estate. But it is important someone takes the lead (excuse the pun). That someone, incidentally, needs to look the part (by which, I don't necessarily mean cravats and tweed waistcoats). It's surprising how much a confident, calm posture rubs off on your dog. If you look as though you're calmly and confidently in charge, you're halfway there.

For situations when a dog cannot be let off-lead, whether it's because they don't yet have good recall or perhaps are recovering from injury, I think a retractable lead can be useful. I'm well aware that many people – dog trainers among them – are vehemently against retractables, but I've come to the conclusion over the years that, when used properly, there should be no problem. Use the locking mechanism to fix the lead at the correct length when you're 'on duty' (and leave it fixed), but release it when you want to declare break time – but only then. Do it right, and you'll have the best of both worlds: a walking lead and a long line.

A word of caution: you need to ensure you buy a good-quality retractable lead. One I've used and find very good is from the German manufacturer, Flexi. Also, when I say break time, I mean when your dog is in a safe space, such as a park where he cannot get onto a road. I worry when I see people walking a dog five metres ahead of them on a pavement. In a moment, that dog could be five metres into a busy road. An owner, then, walking a dog on a retractable lead, is anything but in control.

So, back to Fido. You begin your walk, but all is not well because Fido is pulling like the 09.15 to Euston. The more he pulls, the more you pull back and so it goes on. The problem is a physical reaction has been triggered in both parties. Imagine standing, minding your own business, when a mischievous friend creeps up unnoticed and grabs your coat sleeve, pulling you off-balance to the side. Before you've had the chance to realise what is going on, your nervous system fires into action, sending signals to your muscles, flinging you in the opposite direction.

When dogs are pulling on the lead, it's a chicken and egg situation. Which came first? Did Fido pull and cause his owner to pull back, or was it the other way around? You might be surprised how often it's the latter. Which, of course, is good news. If a person is getting it wrong and triggering a dog problem, that's relatively easy to fix.

Three years ago, I went to see a lady in Solihull in the West Midlands. Pam was a lovely, very sprightly 80-year-old, who had recently lost her husband and had rehomed a boxer/Staffie-cross for company. Griffith was as fit as a fiddle. He wasn't massive, perhaps 30kg, but he was all muscle and a softie by all accounts. He had only one tiny foible. Pam explained that on several occasions that he'd dragged her clean off the pavement and into the path of oncoming traffic on a nearby busy urban dual carriageway. He had a thing for buses and lorries.

We went out walking and arrived at Lode Lane, where every second vehicle seemed to be an articulated lorry taking supplies to the nearby Land Rover factory. I took the lead first, as I often do, and to my surprise Griffith was a perfect gentleman. Not once did he try to throw me under a bus. He didn't pull at all, in any direction.

'Has he always pulled for you?' I asked. I had a hunch.

'Not really. I've had him four months now and he was lovely on a walk to start with. That's why I got him. My last dog was a Border collie and she lunged at anything noisy, like lorries. I was younger then and she was smaller, but I spent every walk holding her back and now it's happening all over again.'

I asked Pam to take the lead and show me, choosing one of the wider sections of the pavement, separated from the carriageway by a broad grass verge. Just as well because, within seconds of taking over, I had to step in and grab the lead to prevent him pulling Pam smack-bang into the path of a double decker bus to Birmingham. It seemed incredible that he hadn't seen it, although the road was lined with trees, and some dogs have no road sense at all. The interesting thing was what had happened just before I stepped in. It wasn't Griffith who had started the pulling at all. It was Pam.

Habit is a powerful thing and years of walking a dog nervous of traffic had made Pam tense up and rein in her dog whenever she saw a large vehicle approaching. Which direction did she pull him? Away from the road, obviously. Which direction did the dog pull away from her? Towards the road. It's obvious when you think about it. From the moment Griffith felt himself being dragged one way, he reacted by pulling the other. With his Land Rover-like low centre of gravity, traction through all four paws, and stump-pulling power, there was only ever going to be one outcome.

Pam and Griffith presented an extreme case, but the moral is clear: even if you think you can win your tug of war, it's best to check that it's not you who is inadvertently starting the struggle in the first place. Give your dog a little slack if you think you're the holding-on-tight type: you may be pleasantly surprised.

A little slack, incidentally, doesn't usually need the lead to be lengthened very much at all. All you need is enough slack to give a J-shape to the lead, as seen from the front when your dog's shoulders are roughly alongside your legs. Give him any more and he can get too far away before you've caught him (or come around the front and trip you up). Much shorter and you risk it being permanently tight.

There's a norm in some circles for a dog to always be on the left of the handler. It's this way in competitions, for example. In the real world of walking pet dogs in town and country, it really doesn't matter, and sticking to the left may not take account of a person's personal preference or need. Arthritis that's worse in the left hand, for example. What I would say is this: pick a side and stick to it. When I see a dog meandering from left to right on a walk, whether it's in front or behind the owner, you can bet your bottom dollar he's used to being on either side of that person and so doesn't know where he's meant to be. If a number of people walk the same dog regularly and have different preferences, that's no problem. Dogs are smart enough to work out that Mum likes left but Dad likes right, for example. There are, as with all rules, exceptions. By all means change sides if you're on a tight road with no pavement in order to keep your dog away from traffic if you judge it's safer, but do revert to normal afterwards and make sure it's the exception, not the rule.

If you're having lead-walking problems, by making a few simple changes you may well find that a walk in the park is as easy as, well, a walk in the park.

Chapter 20

Scared dogs – the Scottish-Mexican and the German-Dane

'I've got a good one for you.' The voice on the phone was my lovely assistant, Sarah. We've been working together for years and I can read the tone of her voice like a book. By 'good', she meant peculiar.

'Oh, aye?'

'Yup. A couple from Scotland who have recently met. They have a dog each, but the dogs aren't getting on. It's stopping them moving in together.'

'Are the dogs fighting?' I asked. Two dogs feuding in a house is always tricky.

'Not really. One is terrified of the other and it's really upsetting for the owners. But here's the thing . . .' I'd been waiting for it – that something out of the ordinary. 'One's a chihuahua called Leia, as in princess, and the other dog . . . have a guess!'

'You're going to tell me it's a big dog, aren't you?' I know her well.

'Yep. It's a Great Dane called Rufus. A chihuahua and a Great Dane! Isn't that brilliant? It's in your diary. Paul and David in Edinburgh. Have fun!'

It was brilliant. I wondered if the dogs had brought them together, perhaps meeting in a park, the poor little chihuahua overwrought with clumping great Rufus, his owner full of apologies. Opposites attract and all that. I'm always interested in people as well as their dogs, and this was fascinating.

'We'll swing by mine and pick up Rufus so you can see them together,' said Paul, as we made our way in his car after he picked me up at the airport. 'Bless him. He's always been a bit of a scaredy cat but he's terrified of Leia.'

'Oh, *he* is scared of *her*? I had it the wrong way around,' I confessed. 'Actually that makes a lot of sense. Danes are usually gentle giants and chihuahuas can be famously feisty.'

'Exactly that. I'd always wanted a Great Dane and I love how placid he is. He wouldn't hurt a fly. I call him Rufus Doofus when we're messing around because it kinda suits him. But I feel so sorry for him. He's five and there's no way I could rehome him. It would break my heart – and his – but when we're at David's he spends all his time either frozen to the spot, running away, or on his back like a submissive puppy, pleading with her not to hurt him, which I know sounds ridiculous.'

'And what about David's dog?' I asked.

'Leia was owned by his grandmother. She passed away and David promised her he would look after her little princess. He's a really big guy, not the chihuahua type at all really, but what can you do? So, that's where you come in, Graeme. We want to move in together – but Rufus is so unhappy near Leia and rehoming either dog isn't an option. I hope you packed your magic wand!'

No pressure, then.

What I saw when we got to David's house explained everything. The man behind the little dog was quite the gentle giant himself (funny how people are sometimes attracted to the human equivalent of their dog). Leia was exactly as advertised, running at a wide-eyed and cowering Rufus, barking her little head off. Even more interesting were Paul and David's reactions.

Paul ran to comfort Rufus by cuddling him and telling him everything was all right. Not that he appeared to believe it himself. He looked anxious (understandable, but of course it rubs off), and although his intention was to reassure with his voice, the words were lost on the poor boy.

'It's OK, Rufus. She won't hurt you.'

Take out the anxiety and Paul's lilting Miss Jean Brodie accent would be perfect for praise in different circumstances but, right then, in Rufus's head, 'It's OK' translated to, 'It's OK to be scared. Do it again and I'll cuddle you more.'

While this was going on, all Rufus could concentrate on was the incoming seek-and-destroy rocket screaming across the sitting room carpet straight towards him, followed by a big man desperately trying to catch up, shouting and screaming (encouragement, presumably, thought Rufus – not that he was going to hang around and find out). Eventually the big man picked up the errant dog-missile, presumably for tactical redeployment another time. It was all utterly, utterly terrifying. Seen through the eyes of a frightened dog, the incongruous situation isn't so hard to understand.

I'm happy to report that, with a little behavioural adjustment (dads, not dogs), the unlikely little and large Scottish, Mexican and German family lived happily ever after. (Germany is where Great Danes – boar-hunting dogs 'of the Danish style' – got their names.)

The Four Fs

During the time I was there, Rufus exhibited three of the classic four Fs of fear: fight, flight, freeze and fawn. We often hear about fight or flight, but not so much the other two.

Rufus took flight, knocking everything out of his way as he did so. He occasionally froze like a larger-than-average-sized rabbit caught in headlights. And when things were calmer he did just as Paul had described in the car: he rolled over like an overgrown puppy, showing his underbelly in a display of fawning to appease Leia. The only F missing – thank goodness – was fight. That would not have ended well.

According to a 2020 study from the University of Helsinki, we may be able to point to genetics for Rufus's fearful tendencies. A team of scientists from the Finnish capital studied the effects of nurture (puppy socialisation and learned responses) and nature (genetics) in a group of 120 Great Danes, identifying anxiety-related genes associated with fearfulness. That's not to say that all Great Danes are born fearful – far from it – but Danes which tend to be easily frightened or anxious may be naturally predisposed to it, despite diligent socialisation and training.

What applies to Great Danes is very likely to apply to other breeds (perhaps even to dog owners too). The Helsinki team concluded there may be shared (genetic) factors underlying anxiety in both humans and dogs. There's a lot of nurture that we can do as owners and trainers, but ultimately we're working with Mother Nature. Both nature and nurture govern dog behaviour. It's never more noticeable than in cases of fearfulness, especially fear-based aggression.

At least Rufus, like most of his breed, wasn't the fighting type. I estimate 80 per cent of the aggression cases I see are fear-based. Those can then be can split into nature (born fearful) or nurture (poor socialisation). Either way, when the penny drops in the dog's mind that acting aggressively often gets rid of the scary dog/man/vehicle, there's every chance the behaviour is set for life without the right interventions.

I wish I had a pound for every time I'd heard that anxiety 'travels down the lead' from owner to dog. It's one of those clichés that masquerades as a truism, except that it's not true at all. How would that work? Is there some kind of dark, mysterious force at play? Or a flow of electrons down the lead? Of course not. Which isn't to say that keeping a tight lead won't make your dog behave badly, because it likely will. Feeling physically restricted and unable to move freely away from the perceived danger is the culprit. Here's an analogy I have for this.

Imagine you're in a pub, in a town you don't know. You've sat down with a drink and realisation begins to dawn that it's a rougher place than it first appeared and the drunk men on the table opposite are arguing ever-more loudly. The atmosphere feels brooding, intimidating. Suddenly a fight erupts in an explosion of smashed beer glasses and tumbling chairs. The voice in your head screams, 'Get out of here, now!' but, before you can slip away unnoticed towards the door, you feel two big hands on your shoulders, pushing you right back into your seat, preventing any possible escape. The message is clear: 'Don't move.' Fear turns to terror. You're trapped.

So it is for a dog on a tightly held lead when they feel – rightly or wrongly – they're in danger. Tethered to a human who's tightening the lead, flight is now impossible. This is not the time to fawn or freeze either, which only leaves one option: to fight.

If you've noticed reactive dogs that are better behaved off-lead than on, in most cases that's why. It's not the lead, or anything magically travelling down it, but tension that's the issue. Given an opportunity not to fight, most fearful dogs don't.

Clearly, I'm not advocating that reactive dogs should be let off-lead and we all hope for the best (although I do think it happens quite a bit, judging from what I see in parks and fields up and down the country). There are better ways of dealing with the problem and, particularly where aggression is involved, there's no substitute for the right hands-on advice.

Not being able to see the frightening thing, but knowing it's still there, is similarly terrifying. Many clients have been told over the years to distract their nervous dog by making them follow a 'watch me' command when, say, another dog appears in the park. The logic seems sound enough initially. If a dog is looking at something, the theory goes, she's thinking about it. True enough. Therefore, if we stop her looking at whatever made her react badly, the idea is she'll stop thinking about it. That's not logical at all. If she's looking, she probably is thinking about it, but making her look away doesn't stop her thinking. It's still there and she knows it, but now she can't see it.

Imagine you're in a park with me on a one-to-one consultation when the local crazed axe-murderer appears on the horizon, screaming, shouting and waving overhead an edged weapon, stained with blood. (I know, it's a bit hyperbolic, but humour me . . .) Imagine if I were to say, 'Oh, dear. Oh, well, don't look at him, pay attention to me, please. I have something important to say.' If you have any sense, you'll ignore me and keep an eye on the dangerous man. Your survival instinct tells you not to take your eye off anything that might hurt you. If I do manage to secure your attention for a few seconds, there's no way on earth you'll be listening to me in any case. He's still there, after all.

So it is with dogs. Forcing a nervous dog to look away from something scary does nothing to reduce her anxiety. On the contrary, it increases, because there's a tension between trying to be a good girl and follow the 'watch me' routine you've trained, and following her instinct to look the other way. Sooner or later when her frustration has built up like a pressure cooker ready to blow, the desperate impulse to protect herself will typically win out in an explosive over-reaction.

It's better to adopt a rule that she can look at anything, but mustn't lunge, bark or try to snap. To teach it, finding the right distance is key. Too close and it's simply impossible for her – and you, probably – to think straight. At the most basic level, forcing a dog to never see things that concern her robs her of the opportunity to learn that most things aren't nearly as scary as they may seem.

Remember our axe murderer? We looked again and it turned out not to be a psychopathic serial killer after all. It was Mr Miggins, the bank manager. He's had a busy day helping people (he hates that) and it's started to rain. Not only is the silver and red umbrella he's requisitioned from the office junior not to his style, but it jammed as he tried to put it up. It's the last straw for Miggins, who's not known for patience at the best of times, and he's now shouting in a fit of pique at the umbrella.

He might be making a lot of noise, but he's probably more of a danger to himself than anyone else. Well, that's a relief. For a moment there, it all seemed very scary. Good job we took a second look.

Chapter 21

Separation anxiety – Maude's monophobia

'It's all right, Maude. I'm only going to school. I'll be back later.'

Ten-year-old Sophie was visibly anxious to be leaving her Jack Russell alone, but closed the front door behind her.

'Come on Sophie, hurry up, we'll be late for school,' her mum shouted through the window of the family car, parked across the street. Time was ticking on. There was a rattling thud at the door, the familiar sound of Maude's front paws pounding against it. And again.

'But Mum . . .'

Sophie opened the door and stepped back in, bending down to reassure the little dog, stroking her on the head. 'I have to go now, Maude. Be a good girl, please.' Her tone suggested something between concern and pleading. She closed the door and turned her back.

Thump.

'Sophie! I'm not going to tell you again!'

Not true, as it turned out, because Sophie couldn't help

herself. She re-opened the door and went through the same process again.

'I can't leave her like this, Mum.' Sophie was close to tears. 'Look, she's upset.'

Her mum got out of the car and walked across the street. Putting her growing unease at the minutes ticking by to one side, she put her arm around Sophie.

'She'll be OK, I promise. Now come on, darling. You've got to go to school and I'm late for work.'

She closed the front door behind them and walked Sophie to the car without moving her arm from Sophie's back. Part caring mum, part arresting officer. As much as she hated this, there was no turning back now. Maude could thump the door all she liked; life had to go on.

Charlotte was a single mum. She'd worked at the hospital all hours God sent to give Sophie the best childhood she could afford. Saving to buy her a puppy had taken months. She'd heard that having a dog was good for children, that it teaches them responsibility and empathy, but as she drove towards the school, hopelessly late once again, she was beginning to regret the decision.

Every day started with the same awful routine: dragging a heartbroken girl to school, tears rolling down her face as she sat crumpled in the passenger seat. What had Charlotte done? Separation anxiety was making life unbearable for everyone.

Everyone except Maude, it turned out. Because although this was in the days before webcams were commonplace, all the evidence pointed to her making the doggy equivalent of a shoulder-shrug once they finally left, wandering about hoovering up the treats on the floor, solving the how-to-get-food-from-a-Kong™ conundrum and then settling down for a nice nap. It's worth remembering a happy dog will sleep all night and much of the day. Certainly, when Charlotte popped back at lunchtime to check on her, she looked sleepy and never appeared anxious.

Like an infant who cries every time she's left at nursery but then stops and plays as soon as the parent leaves, despite appearances, Maude wasn't suffering from separation anxiety at all. Separation anxiety – 'monophobia' – is the fear of being alone. Dogs that suffer from it will often refuse to sleep, eat, drink or do anything resembling normal behaviour for many hours when left alone. Instead, they often pace, bark, howl or cause damage in an effort to escape, often at the entry points of a house.

The most extreme case I've ever seen was in a modern house in Milton Keynes where a recently rehomed Labrador repeatedly burst out of her metal crate and tried, with bleeding paws, to claw and bite her way out of the room by chewing through a plasterboard wall, exposing the mains power cables and plumbing. Thank goodness the owners sought help before she had bitten into the cables or caused a flood, because it was clearly only a matter of time.

Maude wasn't afraid to be alone at all. If anything, she seemed to quite like her own company. What she objected to was people leaving (not unusual with terriers), and had become addicted to the attention she got when they tried to go.

Attention-seeking is not necessarily a sign of separation anxiety, nor is an occasional bark when someone passes by or comes to deliver post. (Not that I'm making light of that.

It's undoubtedly unpleasant for the dog, their would-be victims and the neighbours alike. Not to mention the hapless owners. What's it not, necessarily, is evidence of a dog that's frightened of being left alone.)

For Maude and Sophie the answer was both easy and hard. Ignoring attention-seeking behaviour is often the best solution (provided, as in this case, that there are no underlying anxieties). By repeatedly re-opening the door, Sophie was rewarding Maude's door-thumping behaviour, making it ever worse. The simple answer was, when they left, to create a comfortable environment for Maude, perhaps even take her for a decent walk to help settle her down, but ultimately, when leaving, to just leave. No fuss, no anxious faces, just a quick, matter-of-fact 'See you later' and go. Easy. Except that thinking with your head, not your heart, is often the hardest thing to do of all. Especially when you're ten.

The advent of cheap webcams means we can all now sit at work or in a coffee shop and keep an eye on our dogs via a smartphone. In some cases, we can even choose to be notified every time Fido so much as stretches a leg out of bed. There's nothing wrong with a bit of tech – I like a new gadget myself – but there are downsides. A couple of years ago I had a little heart problem and was under the care of a cardiologist. At the second consultation, I pointed to a shiny new fitness tracker on my wrist. I'd bought it to keep an eye on my heart rate. The good doctor didn't seem very impressed.

'Bad idea?' I asked.

'It depends how you use it,' he said. 'I have patients who buy one, spot a slightly high heart rate and start to worry. Because they are stressed, their heart rate rises, so then they really panic. The heart rate goes through the roof and the next thing you know, they're in A&E.'

I'm inclined to think of dog webcams in the same way: double-edged swords. Not so many years ago, our best tool for figuring out what a home-alone dog was doing was a cassette recorder. Now, we can see and hear everything in real time, and from miles away, too. Not only that, but we can talk to our dogs over the internet.

Therein lies the rub. If you worry every time your dog looks a little restless and press the speaker button to tell him everything's all right and throw in the odd 'good boy' while you're at it, the chances are you'll spook him or, at best, reward the unsettled behaviour. It doesn't take much to trigger a downward spiral of anxious behaviour. He's restless, you react, so then he's more restless and you react even more. Sometimes, as the saying goes, all you have to fear is fear itself.

For serious separation anxiety cases, the issue is often complex – as is the solution. My experience is there's no single remedy, no quick fix. Typically, we'll look at a combination of factors: creating routines designed to get a dog used to being alone for short periods of time; casting an expert eye over the physical environment to see if there are changes that might help him to be more at ease. We may also look at food, perhaps food supplements, that can promote calmness too, and we should certainly consider how interactions with the people in his life are affecting his anxiety.

I'm only scratching the surface here. Books and web articles can be great, but the sheer volume of information available is bewildering. A quick Google search for 'separation anxiety dogs' netted over 14 million results at the time of writing.

If the sheer number of articles on the subject isn't daunting enough, there are also many contradictory points of view to reconcile.

My advice, if you're worried about separation anxiety, is to seek out a trusted professional who can come to your home, make sense of your particular problem and recommend the best combination of strategies for you and your dog, in your environment. Every case is unique.

Chapter 22
Aggression – elephants, dingoes and angry dogs

March 2017. I'm in Sri Lanka in the back of a safari Jeep watching two bull elephants squaring up over a female at a watering hole. One backs down and walks off and the victor spies us. He fixes our group and the tin can we're sitting in with a hard 'What do you think you're looking at?' stare. I'd heard elephants here weren't always friendly – far from it – and sure enough this one's distinctly unhappy. I'm no expert, but I recognise the purposeful, ears-out, coming-to-get-you body language and he starts to lumber toward us. A minute ago, this was all a great show but now we're in trouble. Everyone senses it.

'Can we go now please?' asks a fellow passenger, with a tremble in her voice.

'No,' says Ajith, our park ranger guide, without taking his eyes off the elephant. 'Not yet.' The bull elephant isn't rushing, but his progress towards us is purposeful, relentless, menacing. 'We must stay here,' the ranger adds emphatically.

We sit tight as the elephant approaches the vehicle on the

ranger's side. Just four feet away now, his bulk and weight are only too apparent. He's impressive and frightening at the same time; the Jeep and its miniature occupants seem flimsy. On the one hand, I know this is a moment I'll remember for the rest of my life; on the other, I'm hoping the rest of my life isn't defined in minutes. This isn't Disneyland adrenaline and popcorn scary, it's real dry-mouthed, don't-move-a-muscle, calm-before-the-storm danger.

For several long seconds Ajith waits silently, maintaining eye contact with the elephant until it is so close the animal's hot breath can be felt on his face. This is the moment for action. Ajith shouts loudly. 'Aaaaaah!'

It half works, sending the elephant around to me, at the back of the vehicle. He's so close I could pat him on the head (a very, very bad idea right now, I decide). I copy the ranger's tactic and it works. I'm temporarily pleased with myself until it becomes obvious that our friend has a new plan. He's moved away to the front of the vehicle, but now – lifting a great heavy foot in mid-air – he's threatening to stamp on the bonnet. If he brings that leg down, crushing the engine, we've had it. Seeing the elephant lift his foot, the driver fires up the engine and revs it for all he's worth. It has no effect whatsoever, but then, with a bang, he slams the gear lever forward and throws the Jeep towards the animal in an almighty lurch. And then again, never touching him, but sending out a signal: *Back off!* This is last-ditch desperate.

But finally, it's all over. In slow motion, the elephant turns his massive body and walks away. Not happy, but not fighting. A dignified 'I'll let you off this time' retreat.

'If we had reversed when he first approached,' Ajith tells

me later, at the bar, 'he would have charged. If he thinks you're scared, he thinks he can be brave. Today he wanted to be a hero. When it's like that you have to hold your nerve. Also, don't look away.'

That's easier said than done with a five-ton testosterone-fuelled wannabe hero. We're in a country where 70 people a year are killed in clashes with wild elephants.

I don't know the first thing about angry pachyderms, but I do know a bit about dogs and there are similarities. It's a question of flight or fight. Once an animal is in a dangerously excited state, there are things you can do to influence which way they react. Push too hard and you back your animal into a psychological corner and he'll come out fighting. Back off at the wrong moment – look weak – and you'll risk provoking an attack. Stand your ground, though, which may involve holding a gaze, and you might be surprised by who gives in first, provided you take your time. You should never, ever, rush a dangerously excited animal.

It raises an interesting question about eye contact. I was always told not to make eye contact with an aggressive dog. You may have heard the same. Experience has taught me (and my new ranger chum agreed) that there are times when keeping eye contact with an animal on the edge is key to an outcome where everyone goes home safely. Note, that is eye contact as in gazing or looking, not staring, because, just as it is in the human world, that can be taken as a sign of aggression. Gazing involves soft eyes; stares are hard.

Interestingly, it mirrors an experience I had in Australia a few years earlier when I had the chance to study dingoes briefly on Fraser Island in Queensland. Another park ranger, this time a native Australian guy, told me that I'd be lucky to see a dingo in the forest areas of the island because they'd see me long before I spotted them, and run away.

'But if you do see a dingo close up, holding their ground, you're in big trouble, mate,' he said. It was no exaggeration. At certain times of year when pups were around, a dingo mother will protect her area however she can.

'Your best chance – and there are no guarantees this will save you – is not to run away or try to carry on. Just stand still and, whatever you do, don't take your eyes off her.'

'Stare her out, you mean?' I asked. I was surprised, but he obviously knew his stuff.

'Stare?!' he repeated, incredulous. 'Christ, no! If you stare her out, she'll attack.'

'And if I look away?'

'She'll attack.'

It felt like a tightrope, a little bit too much one way or the other, and you're a goner. Call me a coward, but I resolved not to go walking the forest trails on my own. It didn't seem wise to go upsetting the locals with the wrong kind of look. It did, however, leave a big impression on me. Dingoes are emphatically not pet dogs, but they aren't so far removed genetically, either. What I didn't know at the time was that what I came to call my dingo technique would graphically play out in front of my eyes years later, on a different continent with not a canine, but an elephant. There are perhaps more similarities in the animal kingdom than we appreciate.

So, here's my advice on how best to cope if you're ambushed by a dog (or indeed a dingo or elephant) on your evening walk around the block. There are times when this won't be enough – it wasn't with our elephant and I was very glad to be with an expert at the time – but to stand any chance you should stay calm or at least pretend to be calm. Don't run unless it's a last resort. Don't scream or shout. Don't wave your arms around and, above all else, take your time. Adopt an 'I've got all night' attitude and wait for them to back down. Never take the fight to an angry dog, even if it's only with your eyes.

Chapter 23

Yellow, your new favourite colour?

Aggression is something I'm constantly asked about, so it would be remiss of me not to include it here. But with a caveat – if you're experiencing dog aggression issues, you absolutely shouldn't take everything you read, however well intentioned, as gospel. Every case is different and the advice I may give for one dog might be quite wrong for the next. What follows are a couple of thoughts and a tip of the 'even if it doesn't work it won't make your problem worse' variety.

The majority of aggression cases I see are based in fear, anxiety or nervousness. As we've already seen, like us, when a dog is fearful, she has a choice between backing off (flight) or launching forward (fight). Genetics has a massive influence. Some dogs are born with an inbuilt tendency to be nervous, and the fight/flight (also freeze/fawn) choice is influenced by genetics, too. You'll rarely see an aggressive Newfoundland, for example, but we've all seen shouty terriers.

Think of genetics as a fruitcake; once it's baked and your

raisins have sunk to the bottom, it's too late to rearrange them. So it is with dogs and genes.

A 2020 study of 13,700 dogs from 264 breeds conducted by the University of Helsinki looked into the prevalence of seven anxiety-related traits, including aggression. What holds true for Finnish dogs doesn't necessarily apply in other countries, but the astounding conclusion was that 72.5 per cent of dogs showed 'highly problematic' behaviours.

Although behaviour is usually a combination of nurture and nature, the scientists were especially clear about the genetic link: '*The largest risk ratios were seen between hyperactivity/inattention, separation-related behaviour and compulsion, and between fear and aggression. Furthermore, dog breeds showed large differences . . . suggesting a strong genetic contribution.*'

We can't change nature, but we can work with it. In cases where genetics is the root cause of a behaviour there's no fix or cure, but we can almost always manage things better. That's often achieved by rewarding alternative behaviours.

Often, nervous and reactive dogs need more space. A few years ago, someone had the idea of making yellow the signal colour for dogs that were easily frightened, reactive, were recovering from surgery or for whatever reason needed extra social distance. Wearing a yellow bandana, harness or ribbon tied on a lead indicates: 'I need space, please don't approach.'

The idea took root and it's now internationally recognised. That's great news, but not everyone has heard about it. I went to see someone recently who had a yellow doggy bandana made with the following legend embroidered on it: *My name is Tally. I get nervous. That's why I'm barking.*

Cute, but a lot of words, which meant they were small and barely legible, at least until people were too close, which is pretty ironic really. I suggested a yellow harness: more a dog-sized billboard rather than a place to attach a lead, with just one word written across it, and in much bigger type: *NERVOUS*.

It's not subtle – it's only slightly less visible from space than the Great Wall of China – but it does the job well. People understand at a glance and give Tally the space she needs.

It also has a second, more subtle effect: it changes perceptions. For owners, one of the most upsetting aspects of having a reactive dog is the way other people react to them and their beloved pet. It's not unique to dog parents. A friend, who sometimes works with families of autistic children, saw an interesting parallel when I told her about Tally's case.

'Some parents – particularly mums – really take to heart what other people are thinking about them and their child,' they said. 'I think when someone is judgemental, it touches them at a deep level. I could be quite happy walking down the road with a dog or a child behaving appallingly, and I would just be in my zone and wouldn't care what people think. But the mums I really feel for are the ones who get upset about how others perceive them, because it almost physically hurts.'

Exactly that. People's perceptions, and how they react, can make dog walking unpleasant, even humiliating. It often leads to dogs being walked less which, in turn, doesn't help. A yellow 'nervous' harness changes onlookers' reaction instantly from, 'That's a badly behaved dog/bad owner,' to, 'Bless her, she's nervous.' There's a very handy knock-on effect, too: as we've seen previously in this book, our body language affects our dogs in a big way, and a happier owner often leads to a happier dog. As the end result is more space and considerate onlookers, this leads to a more contented owner and a calmer dog. That's a quadruple whammy, isn't it?

Chapter 24

Caring for dogs with additional needs

Lucy was a very special puppy. She was 14 weeks old when I met her. Her parents had been carefully chosen to combine the best qualities to make her perfect for a very important job – transforming the life of a visually impaired person. Lucy was born to be a guide dog and yet, despite the careful breeding, there was a problem, an insurmountable one. Lucy was blind.

As I drove to her home to meet her and her new owners, Dan and Kirsty, my mind was racing. I'd trained dogs with disabilities before, including dogs that had lost their eyesight, either totally or partially in later life, and dogs that had been blind from birth. I'd helped make the lives of deaf and physically disabled dogs easier too, but this was the first time I'd be starting from scratch with such a young one. I had loads of ideas, but one thing was certain: she'd have to stay on-lead for heelwork. Obviously.

Lucy was utterly adorable: a big ball of yellow fur with an inquisitive streak a mile wide. She was into everything, just like any other puppy, checking out the new person and anything else she could get her mouth around. What was notable from the off was she rarely bumped into anything. Dan and Kirsty had taken a lot of advice from Guide Dogs UK and had made the house puppy-safe. They'd also made a point of not moving things around, which meant that Lucy had mapped out in her head where things were and knew how to avoid them. She was uncannily good at it.

I'd hatched a plan beforehand to train her on the lead to stay with me, using sound so she'd know where I was. Armed with a little jingle bell I'd requisitioned from the Christmas decorations box in my attic, I made a start. I walked slowly at first with the bell tied around my ankle, using the lead to gently guide her if she lagged behind or drifted from me.

Within the time it took Dan to make a mug of tea, Lucy had become my shadow and clearly loved the new game, gambolling along, chasing after me. I started to speed up and change direction, making the turns faster and faster as she got the hang of it. We were both having a high old time.

'Will we always have to walk around with a little bell on, do you think?' Kirsty asked.

It was a good question. Doing Morris dancer impressions isn't for everyone, but it was at least a means to an end. As with humans, when dogs lose one of their senses, the others seem to become more acute to compensate. I took off the bell. It was worth a try.

To my amazement, Lucy carried on playing my catch-me-if-you-can game as though nothing had happened. Perhaps she could hear my footsteps on the soft grass. It could be smell, of course – dogs are famously good with their noses – but her reactions were too quick for that; by the time my scent had wafted away from her, she could have been several feet away. But, no, she was already much more on the ball than that.

'There's your answer,' I shouted across the lawn.

Things were going so incredibly well that I was beginning to think the unthinkable: could Lucy do this without the lead? After all, there was no tension on it now and so it was clear she wasn't relying on the feeling of being attached to me to know where I was. I took it off, called out a quick, 'Come on!' to give her a fighting chance and set off, a little slower than before.

I needn't have been so cautious. Lucy was going great guns, as though this was the best challenge in the world. I sped up, slowed down, stopped dead, turned abruptly away from her and every time her reaction was instant as she followed me relentlessly, like a heat-seeking missile.

How did she do it? Truth be told, I'm not entirely sure. Hearing is probably the best conventional explanation and, although I was being quiet, it's entirely possible she could hear my footsteps and my breath. But her reactions were so quick, as if she had some bat-like sonar or sixth sense superpower and knew exactly where I was. At the risk of sounding terribly woo-woo, I'm convinced there's something more than we can explain scientifically – at least with the knowledge we currently have. We know a lot about dogs, but still there's so much to discover.

I've had some astounding experiences over the years with dogs that live with all manner of disabilities. The one thing they have in common is that they don't see themselves as disadvantaged at all, whether they were born disabled or became disabled later in life. From deaf dogs that expertly read hand signals to the three-legged lurcher that could outrun all the other dogs in the park – if we focus on what they can do, instead of their limitations, they adapt amazingly quickly.

'You can't teach an old dog new tricks' is one of those truisms that's repeated so often you'd be forgiven for thinking it must be true. It's not. Older dogs, like older people, are quite capable of learning new things. Not only is it possible, but keeping the brain active is a very good thing indeed. 'Use it or lose it' might be a better adage to keep in mind.

Take collie-cross Teddy, for example. He was ten years old when he was rescued by the RSPCA from the only home he'd ever known. It wasn't the kind of home most dogs are used to. This was one of those stories that occasionally hit the news: a large number of dogs living in a house start multiplying to the point where the owner has lost control and they end up being taken away. The elderly lady who owned the large country house and grounds where he'd lived thought she had 27 dogs. The final count was more than 50. They were well fed – Waitrose deliveries, no less – but were, to all intents and purposes, feral.

Teddy was a sweetheart, but when I met him at his new home he ran into the back garden and stayed there for three hours. He was terrified of anything new, including me. He was so timid that to get him to eat, owners Greg and Marianne had either to go outside when the bowl went down or hide away on the third floor of their townhouse. It wasn't so surprising because, for ten years, he hadn't left the place where he was born. He'd not seen the outside world, never worn a collar or harness, never been to the vets, and never seen a stranger apart from the driver of the big green van who came and went.

'He never sits,' said Greg. 'I don't mean sit still or sit on command. We've literally never seen him sit since we got him.'

We take it for granted that all dogs sit. That's because pretty much every dog we've ever seen grew up with humans around them. Puppies look up to humans (literally) and their muscles are relatively weak. Frequently they rest their bottoms on the floor when they look at us (sometimes we train it specifically, other times it happens by accident). When they do, we smile and tell them what a clever puppy they are. Give them a treat, and Bob's your uncle: a habit is formed.

Teddy never got the memo. He was either lying, standing, walking or (rarely, until we taught him recall) running, but never sitting. It's a mark of how much he had to learn, starting from the age equivalent of when humans draw a pension.

There was a lot to do and all in a purely positive way. Greg and Marianne were patient and persistent. I chatted on the phone a few times about progress in the following weeks until the calls naturally petered out. Then, about six months after we'd first met, the phone rang and it was Greg. I'd saved his number.

'Hi, Greg. Everything OK?' I had an uneasy feeling. It had been a while and Teddy was an old dog, after all.

'Yes, absolutely fine,' he said. 'I thought I'd give you a progress report.'

That was a relief.

'I've just got back from the park and something dawned on me. Teddy was running around chasing a ball and playing with his mates, having a whale of a time, and I realised

I'd started to take it all for granted. I mean, he'd never seen a ball – he was scared of them when you first met him. Anyway – long story short – I called to tell you something.'

'OK . . .?'

'Teddy's a normal dog now. Normal! Isn't that great?'

Normal. It's one of my fondest memories from the last decade. I had been sure the old dog could learn a few new tricks, but what I never foresaw was a day when normal would be amazing.

Chapter 25

The end of life

And so we come, inexorably, to the end of life. 'In this world, nothing is certain except death and taxes,' are words most usually attributed to Benjamin Franklin. He was right, of course. Dogs fare better than their people on the tax front, but death is somewhat trickier. None of us is getting out of here alive. The fact is humans live much longer than dogs, which in turn means that almost all dog lovers experience the loss of a pet sooner or later, often repeatedly.

Bereavement is a difficult subject. There are, I suppose, no absolute rights or wrongs. We all – humans and dogs – deal with it in our own way. What I offer here are a few words of advice that I've picked up from thousands of conversations with dog owners over the years. They helped me through some pretty tough times.

A conversation I had with a client in the early days made a huge impression on me. We started talking about the family's older dog, a Labrador, that had lived to a ripe old age and been put to sleep by the vet in the back garden of the family home.

'Millie loved lying on this patio,' her owner explained.

'She'd stay here for hours, sunbathing. So, when the time came, we brought her here and she left us surrounded by the whole family, stroking her and loving her. I gave her some chocolate earlier that morning because she'd spent her whole life trying to eat ours and we never let her. It hardly mattered at this stage, so she got her first taste on her last day. It was sad to say goodbye, but it was a lovely way to do it.'

At the time, I'd never heard of a vet coming out for this reason, but it made so much sense to me. I'm convinced it's better for both the dog and the family. Axel and Gordon were young at the time – barely puppies – but I vowed that this would be the way I would do it, if it were possible, come the time. As it turned out, that's how it was.

Having more than one dog poses another question: how best to help the surviving dogs when another dies? I've heard so many stories over the years of a poorly dog being taken away to the vets, never to return, and it leading to the remaining dog pining for weeks or months. It seems particularly to happen when there's only one dog left. They'll look out of windows and sniff at doors, seemingly searching for the missing dog which will, of course, never come back. It's traumatic for everyone, not least the dog.

On the other hand, I've also heard many stories of dogs seeing the body of one that had died and instinctively understanding. I'm not aware of any science behind it, but I've become convinced there's something in it, that it does help them move on. It is, after all, nature's way.

When the time came for me to say goodbye to Axel and Gordon, I was grateful for the opportunity to let them go at home. I was then – still am – writing a monthly column in

Countryside magazine and so I wrote about the journey at the time. I've decided to reproduce those columns here in the hope they may help others through those darkest hours of sharing life with a dog.

A Big-Hearted Dog (July 2016)

I'm on first-name terms with my vet these days. Which is nice, but not good. Hugo's a congenial man – and as far as I can tell a brilliant vet – but I'd much rather I didn't know him quite so well. It's what comes from having two older dogs.

I dropped ten-year-old Axel off for a quick routine procedure the other day, but the phone rang before I'd got home.

'Graeme, it's Hugo. Axel's heart rate is through the roof. Something is wrong. If this is what I think it is, his other issues can wait. Let me scan his heart and I'll call you.'

It had been a fairly ordinary day but now, suddenly, it wasn't. There was no way back. A dark, tar-heavy foreboding dragged me down and I could think of nothing else until the call came, the moment of inevitable truth.

Dilated cardiomyopathy. Axel had an enlarged heart that didn't work properly, and it could only get worse. There was some treatment, but no cure.

Axel is a big-hearted boy, a gentle giant who wins over everyone he meets. That's quite a talent for a 50kg so-called devil dog. And here he was, slowly dying of an enlarged heart. The irony was physically painful.

I couldn't wait to pick him up, but I was apprehensive of what I'd find. I was fearful, too, of my own emotions, how I'd react. When I arrived, he looked very sorry for himself, half-drugged from anaesthetics, with several patches shaved in his thick black fur. I put my hand on the back of his neck and ruffled his fur with my fingertips to reassure him. It did little to reassure me. I blamed myself. He'd been a bit lethargic recently. It had been such a gradual decline and I'd been too damned busy to notice it.

'You couldn't have prevented it,' said Hugo, as if he'd read my mind. No doubt he'd been here many times before with others. 'Some breeds are susceptible to it. It's really hard to spot. Remember, I didn't suspect it until I checked his heart rate this morning.' He's a kind man.

Axel's been at my side through a lot over the last ten years. It's been quite a rollercoaster. He and Gordon have been my only constants. We've been the Three Musketeers for so long. I've been the man with the two Rottweilers wherever I've lived and they've been the Dogfather's dogs. But all good things come to an end and a time for mourning is fast approaching.

I'm dreading it.

Axel, 2005–2016 (October 2016)

I was touched by the response to my article a couple of months ago when I wrote about Axel's heart condition. I thought you'd want to know that we said goodbye in late September.

Everyone says you know when the time has come. For a few days, he'd been weak, but still willing to try to live a normal life. The spark was still there until one day he decided he didn't really want to get up at all. He'd given up trying and just wanted to sleep.

Perhaps it seems odd to say, but making the decision was

easy. The hardest thing was calling the vet. I rehearsed the script in my head, dialled the number and everything was fine until I had to ask for what I wanted. Much as it was the right thing, I didn't actually want it at all.

'Could you please send ...' I said, and then – abruptly – nothing. A choking silence replaced my voice as head and heart crashed together. Tears started to quietly splash, one by one, onto the tiles of the kitchen floor where Axel lay at my feet. The thought was too shocking, the words, quite literally, unspeakable.

'Bless you,' said the receptionist. I suppose they recognise the lack of sound when grown men cry at the end of the phone. 'Would you like me to ask Hugo if he can come out?'

Axel died peacefully at home, surrounded by love. Gordon came back in the room after he'd passed away, took one look, decided that was that, looked at me as if to say, 'I see Axel's dead, then?' and went to play with his friend, Hugo. Dogs cope better than we do. I didn't know whether to laugh or cry. I did both, in quick succession.

So, farewell Axel, old friend. A decade feels like a heartbeat now it's over. It was an honour to share life with you and learn so much from you. Maybe one day we'll meet again, but for now, sleep well. My big-hearted boy.

The Last Thing (July 2017)

I really thought it would be a couple of years before I'd be writing this. Regular readers will remember I lost my big-hearted Rottweiler, Axel, late last year. He was survived by Gordon, not much younger, but as fit as a fiddle.

Gordon coped well without Axel. He was a little subdued for a week or so and then he bounced back. Literally. He'd never been in kennels on his own, so on the first occasion I asked kennel boss, Darryl, to ring me if there was a problem. The call never came.

'Has he been OK?' I asked tentatively, when I arrived to collect him.

'OK? He's more than OK,' said Darryl. 'Every time I let him out in the paddock, he bounces around like bloody Bambi!'

I knew that bounce: Gordon, my cheeky chap, full of the joys of life.

And so he continued, bouncing through Christmas into the New Year, through his annual vet's health check in February ('He's in great shape for an old Rottie. See you next year'). So it was, until four weeks ago, when I realised the bouncing had stopped. He didn't seem ill exactly, but at some point, when no one was looking, Bambi had left the building.

Mindful of Axel's slow decline, I took Gordon to the vet's, just to be on the safe side. Twenty-four hours, one ultrasound, an X-ray and a sheaf of blood tests later we had a diagnosis. It wasn't good news. My memory of the conversation is a little blurry. I really hadn't seen this coming at all.

'Tumours in at least three sites . . . possibly in his brain . . . in a lot of pain . . . impossible to give a timescale . . . palliative care.'

Palliative care! I only brought him in to be checked out and fixed up for another couple of years. And in pain, too. I had no idea. Poor, poor Gordon. Some dogs mask it so well.

There was an alternative. Put him through a series of tests leading to chemo, which might extend his life, studies suggested, by an average of 28 days. But 28 days of what, exactly?

He'd lived almost 11 years as cheeky, happy Gordon and it's not as though I could buy him four weeks of youthful happiness.

My instinct, of course, was to keep him going as long as I could – what dog lover wouldn't? But for whose benefit would that be? For his or mine? Ultimately, given a choice between fighting the inevitable or keeping him pain-free for as long as we had left, palliative care was – perhaps surprisingly – an easy decision.

It turned out we didn't have long together. The vet visit had been on a Thursday. Over the weekend he started bumping into things, vomiting occasionally, not eating. We adjusted the medication, but it made no difference, and on Tuesday morning I let him go. It happened on the same floor, in the same kitchen, with the same vet, as Axel.

And yet, it was different. I used to think that they always let you know; that, like Axel, they somehow communicate: 'I've had enough, please let me sleep.'

But not Gordon. He kept trying to drunkenly walk around the garden to show me he was all right, which he clearly wasn't. It was heart-breaking to watch. The decline was stunningly fast. He was visibly worsening by the hour. Even then, between bouts of fitting as the cancer in his head took over, he tried again and again to brush things off. 'I'm OK, Dad. You'll see. I'm not done yet.' But he was.

Don't let anyone tell you dogs always know when it's time to go. The brutal truth is sometimes they don't. That's when it falls to us. With indescribable sadness, I made my awful decision. I loved my dog. I always will. It was the last thing I could do for him.

Goodbye Gordon, cheeky chap, Bambi impersonator. Born 2006, bounced off this mortal coil on 11 July 2017.

* * *

When the inevitable time comes to say goodbye, we must think not about what's best for us, but what's right for our dog. For a lifetime of love and companionship, for all the laughs and cuddles, it's the least we can do. Think with your head. Your heart will follow.

There's a quote that often comes to mind when I remember my boys: *Grief is the price we pay for love.*

Epilogue

Bonkers problems

I wanted this book to reflect a whole life with a dog: from the moment you bring home a puppy, to the heartbreaking day when you have to say goodbye. But, that presented something of a problem, as I didn't want to leave you sobbing into your tea. Instead, I thought I'd leave you with a smile on your face with this short section I've called 'Bonkers Problems'. They're the weird and wonderful enquiries I've received over the years that either have the simplest solution in the world or are totally impossible to fix. Read on and you'll see why.

They are the outtakes or bloopers of real life. Often someone will get in touch with a problem that has the easiest, most obvious of fixes, but one that they've never considered. I know I'm doing myself out of a job by giving two minutes of advice, but it's worth it to hear the relief in their voices.

The others are issues I would defy any dog trainer (or indeed certified genius) to fix. There is no solution, but they illustrate that the life of a dog trainer is filled with both the sublime and the ridiculous.

You've got mail . . .

Them: I've got a dog.

Me: Good start.

Them: He's absolutely perfect in every way apart from the fact he eats the post. We're not here when it arrives and he's chewed up cheques, two passports and a couple of debit cards. What can we do?

Me: There's a really long-winded dog psychology answer or there's a ten-minute practical fix. You know those metal letterboxes that go outside the house . . . ?

Them: Oh my God, you're a marvel.

Me: We aim to please.

Music to my ears . . .

Them: Please help. We love *Coronation Street* but every time the music comes on our dog goes bananas, barking and shouting. Even if he's in the other room, he hears the tune and starts kicking off.

Me: You know that button on your remote control that mutes the sound?

Them: Yes . . .

Me: Press it and don't turn the sound back on until the titles are over.

Them: Wow, brilliant. How did we never think of that?

A tight spot . . .

Them: When I come in from work, my dog jumps all over me. I've lost count of the number of pairs of tights he's gone through. Oddly, he never does it to my husband.

Me: What do you do when you get in?

Them: I fuss him because I love him.

Me: What does your husband do when he gets in?

Them: He ignores the dog, the ignorant man.

Me: How many pairs of tights has your husband had ruined?

Them: None.

Me: Uh-huh . . .

The language of love

Them: I rescued a dog from Spain. Do I have to speak Spanish to him?

Me: Sí.

Them: Really?

Me: No.

Them: Was that Spanish "no"?

Me: No. Seriously, a command can be anything you like. It just has to be consistent. You can say "sit" in any language you like as long as it's always the same word you use. ¡Olé!

Even dogs have a view on Brexit . . .

Them: Our dog knows the word for biscuit, but his hearing isn't so great. So, every time he hears the word "Brexit" he whines for a treat. He's getting a little fat now. What can we do?

Me: Try saying, 'leaving the EU'.

Them: Ha ha. Perfect!

(Don't feed people-biscuits to your dog, incidentally – you knew that, right?)

And then there are the problems that are way above my pay grade. One of my favourite enquiries of all time went something like this . . .

Them: Can you train my dog not to snore at night?

Me: Is he asleep at the time?

Them: Well, yeah.

Me: Hmm. I've trained more than 5,000 dogs, but they were all awake at the time, so no, I might be struggling with that.

Since I've been on the telly, people think I have amazing powers I definitely do not possess. They include a man from Northern Ireland who seemed to think I am psychic. This is the email I got from my assistant.

Lost dogs

A gentleman called to say his two dogs were taken into a free kennel while he was in hospital. His neighbour helped him arrange it; however, they called so many places they cannot remember where the dogs went. He is wondering if you would know. Please advise.

Obviously, I couldn't leave it there. I had to know more so I rang him.

He seemed surprised that I might not have the information at the tip of my fingers, but went on to share more of the story. He had two dogs that went to the kennels, but he wasn't very bothered about getting the larger one back. The small one, on the other hand, whom he described as 'a lovely little fellow', he very much wanted to be reunited with, if I could be so kind as to arrange this. I suggested he got in touch with the local newspaper to put out an appeal. Sadly, I never did find out what happened.

Wasting money

I may have mentioned (once or twice before) that I'm a Yorkshireman, which means I cannot abide the idea of wasting money. It's why I am endlessly perplexed when people call to book a consultation utterly convinced that I will not be able fix their problem.

A case in point was a call one Wednesday afternoon: 'To be honest, I don't believe you can sort out these bad dogs on the TV within a couple of hours. I'd be most surprised if you could do it with my daughter's dog. There's no way within a couple of hours you could possibly sort Betty out.'

I'm never quite sure what to say in a case like this one. I once spent four hours with a man and his troublesome Cairn terrier in the Lake District. We had a really good day and everything went well with the training.

'Worth every penny,' he said, handing me his credit card to settle the not insubstantial bill. Then he added: 'I'll tell you what, I didn't think for one minute you'd be able to do it, but I was wrong – he's like a different dog.'

It never ceases to amaze me that people occasionally book me feeling that there's no way I will be able to help, but are happy to waste money proving it. It's an extraordinary thing that I think only applies to dog training. After all, never in the history of dentistry has anyone called a dentist and said, 'I don't believe there's any way in the world that you could fix my toothache but I'd like to throw a load of money at you anyway.'

My advice to anyone faced with a problem – be it a badly behaved dog or anything else – is to think positively.

To misquote someone wiser than me: 'Whether you think you CAN do something or you think you CAN'T, either way you're probably right.'

It's great thinking. I apply it with all dogs . . . great and small.

Acknowledgements

It takes a heck of a lot of people to put a book together and I want to say a huge thank you to the teams at Penguin and M & C Saatchi Merlin for being there every step of the way and helping bring this book into the world.

None of it could have been written without those I've met along the way who have allowed me into their lives and have trusted me to help with their problems. It's a huge privilege to be able to help bring harmony into homes for such amazing dogs and their people. The vast majority of people I meet have boundless love for their dogs and I hope these stories show that.

Index

GH indicates Graeme Hall.